D0900106

THE INTERPRETATION OF
FINANCIAL STATEMENTS

The Interpretation of Financial Statements

BY

BENJAMIN GRAHAM

AND

CHARLES McGOLRICK

A revision of the book
by Benjamin Graham and
Spencer B. Meredith
first published in 1937

HARPER & ROW, PUBLISHERS
New York and Evanston

CONTENTS

PREFACE   vii

PART I

BALANCE SHEETS AND INCOME ACCOUNTS

I. FINANCIAL STATEMENTS IN GENERAL	1
II. BALANCE SHEETS IN GENERAL	2
III. TOTAL ASSETS AND TOTAL LIABILITIES	5
IV. CAPITAL AND SURPLUS	7
V. CURRENT ASSETS	9
VI. CURRENT LIABILITIES	11
VII. WORKING CAPITAL	12
VIII. CURRENT RATIO	16
IX. CASH	19
X. RECEIVABLES	21
XI. INVENTORIES	23
XII. CURRENT LIABILITIES (NOTES PAYABLE)	27
XIII. PROPERTY ACCOUNT (FIXED ASSETS)	29
XIV. DEPRECIATION AND DEPLETION IN THE BALANCE SHEET	31
XV. NONCURRENT INVESTMENTS (INTERMEDIATE ASSETS)	33
XVI. INTANGIBLE ASSETS	35
XVII. PREPAID EXPENSE AND DEFERRED CHARGES	37
XVIII. RESERVES	39

XIX. Book Value or Equity 42

XX. Calculating Book Value 44

XXI. Tangible Asset Protection for Bonds and Preferred Stocks 46

XXII. Other Items in Computing Book Value 48

XXIII. Liquidating Value and Net Current Asset Value 49

XXIV. Earning Power 50

XXV. A Typical Public Utility Income Account 51

XXVI. A Typical Railroad Income Account 54

XXVII. A Model Industrial Income Account 56

XXVIII. Calculating Earnings 57

XXIX. The Safety of Fixed Charges and Preferred Dividends 60

XXX. Maintenance, Depreciation, and Similar Factors in the Income Account 62

XXXI. The Trend of Earnings 67

XXXII. Common Stock Prices and Values 68

XXXIII. Conclusion 70

Part II

Debits and Credits 73

Part III

Analyzing a Balance Sheet and Income Account by the Ratio Method 77

Part IV

Definitions of Financial Terms and Phrases 85

Preface

THIS BOOK is designed to enable you to read financial statements intelligently. Financial statements are intended to give an accurate picture of a company's condition and operating results, in a condensed form. Everyone who comes in contact with corporations and their securities has occasion to read balance sheets and income statements. Every business man and investor is expected to be able to understand these corporation statements. For security salesmen and for customers' brokers in particular, the ability to analyze statements is essential. When you know what the figures mean, you have a sound basis for good business judgment.

Our plan of procedure is to deal successively with the elements that enter into the typical balance sheet and income account. We intend first to make clear what is meant by the particular term or expression, and then to comment briefly upon its significance in the general picture. Wherever possible we shall suggest simple standards or tests which the investor may use to determine whether a company's showing in a given respect is favorable or the reverse. Much of this material may appear rather elementary, but even in the elementary aspects of the subject there are peculiarities and pitfalls which it is important to recognize and guard against.

Of course the success of an investment depends ultimately upon future developments, and the future may never be "analyzed" with accuracy. But if you have precise information as to a company's present financial position and its past earnings record, you are better equipped to gauge its future possibilities. And this is the essential function and value of security analysis.

The material in this book is designed either for independent study as an elementary work or as an introduction to a more detailed treatment of the subject—such as *Security Analysis* by Benjamin Graham and David L. Dodd (McGraw-Hill, 1951). In the present revised version of the original 1937 edition, an effort has been made to bring the treatment and illustrations up to date. Considerable use is made of the recently available composite Financial Reports of United States Manufacturing Corporations, published jointly by the Federal Trade Commission and the Securities & Exchange Commission.

B. G.
C. McG.

New York City
March, 1955

THE INTERPRETATION OF
FINANCIAL STATEMENTS

CHAPTER I

Financial Statements in General

A FULL financial statement contains two major parts: an income account and a balance sheet. The income account shows the earnings for the period covered, while the balance sheet sets forth "the financial position" at the closing date. The company's report may include additional statements and supplementary schedules, such as an analysis of changes in capital and surplus, a summary of the "cash flow," and others.

The annual report is issued as of the close of the company's fiscal year. In the majority of cases this is December 31, but a large number of businesses select some other date. This would generally be after the close of the active season, when inventories and current liabilities are likely to be at a low point.

In addition to the annual report, nearly all concerns issue interim statements, usually containing the earnings only, but sometimes including the balance sheet as well. Monthly figures are available for all railroads and most public utilities. Other businesses—referred to for convenience as "industrials"—for the most part publish their results quarterly.

CHAPTER II

Balance Sheets in General

A BALANCE sheet shows how a company stands at a given moment. There is no such thing as a balance sheet covering the year 1954; it can be for only a single date, for example, December 31, 1954. A single balance sheet may give some indications as to the company's past performance, but this may be studied intelligently only in the income accounts and by a comparison of successive balance sheets.

The function of the balance sheet is to show what the company owns and what it owes. In the form of the balance sheet now in general use all the items owned are listed in a left column and called the assets. The liabilities—what the company owes—are listed in a column to the right.

The assets include money the company holds or has invested, money owed to it by others, and the physical properties. Sometimes there are also intangible assets, such as good will, which are frequently given an arbitrary value.

The liability side lists all the debts of the corporation and the equity or ownership interest of the stockholders. Debts incurred in the operation of the business appear as accounts payable. The more formal borrowings are listed as bonds or notes outstanding. Reserves of various kinds may also be listed as liabilities.

The stockholders' interest is called capital and surplus. These are liabilities only in the sense that they represent the amount for which the company is responsible to the stockholders. More truly, they are the arithmetical difference between the assets and the liabilities, and they are placed among the liabilities to bring the "balance sheet" into balance.

A balance sheet in the typical form:

Assets	$5,000,000	Liabilities	$4,000,000
		Capital & surplus	1,000,000
	$5,000,000		$5,000,000

really means:

Assets	$5,000,000
Less liabilities	4,000,000
Stockholders' interest	$1,000,000

The balance sheet presented below is taken from the quarterly financial reports published by the Federal Trade Commission and the Securities and Exchange Commission, covering United States manufacturing corporations. It shows the combined assets and liabilities of about 9,000 companies at the end of 1953.

BALANCE SHEET
(*millions of dollars*)

Assets		*Liabilities & Stockholders' Equity*	
Cash & U.S. gov't securities	$28,287	Short-term loans payable	$ 6,081
Accts. rec.	22,829	Accts. payable	14,873
Inventories	44,967	Income taxes accrued	13,873
Other current assets	2,389	Other current liabilities	7,490
Total current assets	98,472	Total current liabilities	42,317
Property, plant, & equipment	112,614	Long-term bank loans & debt	18,082
		Other noncurrent liabilities	1,456
Less reserve for depreciation & depletion	50,208		
	62,406		
Other noncurrent assets	10,363	Miscellaneous reserves	2,181
		Capital	45,594
		Surplus	61,611
Total assets	$171,241	Total liabilities & equity	$171,241

New and more informing methods of presentation of the balance sheet figures are gradually becoming popular in corporate statements. The annual report of the U.S. Steel Corporation presents the information as a "Statement of Financial Position." This is a single column of figures, which arrives at the stockholders' investment by deducting the liabilities from the assets.

U.S. STEEL CORPORATION

CONSOLIDATED STATEMENT OF FINANCIAL POSITION

December 31, 1953

Current assets	
Cash	$ 214,595,340
United States government securities	217,320,480
Receivables	237,001,416
Inventories	505,409,401
Total	1,174,326,637
Less:	
Current liabilities	
Accounts payable	323,709,804
Accrued taxes	474,095,788
Dividends payable	25,887,237
Long-term debt due in one year	4,614,023
Total	828,306,852
Working capital	346,019,785
Miscellaneous investments	22,449,287
Plant and equipment, less depreciation	1,970,002,353
Operating parts and supplies	55,213,949
Costs applicable to the future	25,508,740
Total assets less current liabilities	2,419,194,114
Deduct:	
Long-term debt	64,475,699
Reserve for insurance, contingencies and miscellaneous expense	100,061,875
Excess of assets over liabilities and reserves	$2,254,656,540
Ownership evidenced by	
Preferred stock 7% ($100 par), 3,602,811 shares	$360,281,100
Common stock, 26,109,756 shares	
Stated value $33⅓ per share $870,325,200	
Income reinvested 1,024,050,240	1,894,375,440
Total	$2,254,656,540

CHAPTER III

Total Assets and Total Liabilities

THE totals of assets and liabilities appearing on the balance sheet supply a rough indication of the size of the company. Years ago it was customary to inflate the assets by including a large amount of fictitious "good will," either as a separate item or by merely including it with the property account. This practice is now all but extinct. To some extent the contrary situation prevails today, since in many cases the property-account figure shown on the statement is far below its current replacement value. It is also true that many companies possess valuable patents, trade-marks, and ordinary good will which are not reflected in the asset account.

The size of a company may be measured in terms either of its assets or of its sales. In both cases the significance of the figure is entirely relative, and must be judged against the background of the industry. The assets of a small railroad will exceed those of a good-sized department store. From the investment standpoint, especially that of the buyer of high-grade bonds or preferred stocks, it may be well to attach considerable importance to large size. This would be true particularly in the case of industrial companies, for in this field the smaller enterprise is more subject to sudden adversity than is likely in a railroad or public utility. Where the purchase is made for speculative profit, or long-term capital gains, it is not so essential to insist upon dominant size, for there are countless examples of smaller companies prospering more than large ones. After all, the large companies themselves presented the best speculative opportunities while they were still comparatively small.

CHAPTER IV

Capital and Surplus

THE interest or equity of the stockholders in the business, as shown by the books, is represented by capital and surplus. In the typical case, the money paid in by the stockholders is designated as capital, and the profits not paid out as dividends make up the surplus (or "reinvested earnings"). The capital is represented by shares of stock, sometimes of only one kind or class, sometimes of various kinds, which are usually called preferred and common. Other titles have also come into use, such as Class A or Class B, deferred shares, founders' shares, etc. The rights and limitations of various kinds of stock cannot safely be inferred from their title, but the facts must be definitely ascertained from the charter provisions, which in turn are summarized in the investors' manuals or other statistical records and reference books.

The shares may be either of a definite par value or without par. In the simple case the par value shows how much capital was paid in for each share by the original subscribers to the stock. A company with one million shares, par $100, would presumably represent a far greater investment than another company with one million shares, par $5. However, in the modern corporate setup neither the par value nor the total dollar value of the capital stock may be in the slightest degree informing. The capital figure is frequently stated at much less than the actual amount paid in by the stockholders, the balance of their contribution being stated as some form of surplus. The shares themselves may be given no par value, which means theoretically that they represent no particular amount of money contribution, but rather a certain fractional interest in the total equity. In many cases nowadays, a low par value is arbitrarily assigned to the shares, largely to reduce incorporation fees and transfer taxes.

These various practices may be illustrated by assuming that the stockholders of a company pay in $10,000,000 in exchange for 100,000 shares of capital stock. Under former procedure the shares would undoubtedly have been given a par value of $100, and the balance sheet would have shown the following:

Capital, 100,000 shares, par $100 $10,000,000

More recently, the shares might have been given no par value, and the entry would have read:

Capital, 100,000 shares, no par. Stated value $10,000,000

Or the incorporators might have decided arbitrarily to state the capital at a smaller figure, say one-half of the amount paid in. In that case, the entries would read:

Capital, 100,000 shares, no par. Stated value $5,000,000
Capital surplus (or paid-in surplus) $5,000,000

The most "modern" arrangement would be to give the shares an arbitrarily low par, say $5. Hence we would see the following peculiar balance sheet setup:

Capital, 100,000 shares, par $5 $ 500,000
Capital surplus   9,500,000

In present-day balance sheets, therefore, the division between capital and surplus may be quite meaningless. For most purposes of analysis it is best to take the capital and the various kinds of surplus items together, giving a simple figure for the total equity of the stockholders.

CHAPTER V

Current Assets

CURRENT assets are those which are immediately convertible into cash or which, in the due course of business, tend to be converted into cash within a reasonably short time. (The limit usually set is a year.) Sometimes they are called liquid or quick or floating assets. Current assets group themselves into three broad classes: (1) cash and its equivalents; (2) receivables, i.e., money which is due to the company for goods or services sold; or (3) inventories held for sale or for the purpose of conversion into goods or services to be sold. In the operation of the business these assets change gradually into cash. For example, in a later balance sheet the present inventory would have become cash and receivables, while the present receivables would probably have become cash. Current assets are usually shown on the balance sheet in the relative order of their liquidity.

To give the picture in somewhat more detail, the following list of current asset items is shown, grouped for convenience into the three classes mentioned above.

1. Cash and equivalent:
    Cash on hand or in bank
    Special deposits
    Government and municipal securities
    Other marketable securities

2. Receivables:
    Accounts receivable

        Notes receivable
        Interest receivable
        Due from agents

3. Inventories:
        Finished goods ("salable")
        Work in progress ("convertible")
        Materials and supplies ("consumable")

Certain kinds of receivables may be relatively noncurrent —e.g., amounts due from officers and employees, including stock subscriptions. If such accounts are not due to be received by the company within a year, they are usually shown separately from the current assets.

On the other hand, it is customary to include the full amount of installment accounts receivable in the current assets, even though a good part may be due later than one year from the date of the balance sheet. Similarly, the entire merchandise inventory is included in the current assets, although some of the items may be slow moving.

CHAPTER VII

Working Capital

IN STUDYING what is called the "current position" of an enterprise, we never consider the current assets by themselves, but only in relation to the current liabilities. The current position involves two important factors: (1) the excess of current assets over current liabilities, known as the net current assets or the working capital, and (2) the ratio of current assets to current liabilities, known as the current ratio.

The working capital is found by subtracting the current liabilities from the current assets. Working capital is a consideration of major importance in determining the financial strength of an industrial enterprise, and it deserves attention also in the analysis of public utility and railroad securities.

In the working capital is found the measure of the company's ability to carry on its normal business comfortably and without financial stringency, to expand its operations without the need of new financing, and to meet emergencies and losses without disaster. The investment in plant account (or fixed assets) is of little aid in meeting these demands. Shortage of working capital, at its very least, results in slow payment of bills with attendant poor credit rating, in curtailment of operations and rejection of desirable business, and in a general inability to "turn around" and make progress. Its more serious consequence is insolvency and the bankruptcy court.

The proper amount of working capital will vary with the

volume of sales and the type of business. The chief point of comparison is the amount of working capital per dollar of sales. Food companies in 1953, for example, doing essentially a cash business and enjoying a rapid turnover of inventory, will have high sales per dollar of working capital. But tobacco companies, which must hold their inventories for a three-year "curing" period, need large working capital in relation to sales.

NET SALES PER DOLLAR OF WORKING CAPITAL OF UNITED STATES MANUFACTURING CORPORATIONS[a]

December 31, 1953

	Net Sales	Working Capital	Net Sales per $ of Working Capital
	(billions of dollars)		
All industries	$265.9	$56.2	$4.73
Food	42.6	6.0	7.10
Tobacco manufacturers	3.8	1.9	2.00
Textile mill products	13.0	3.4	3.82
Apparel and finished textiles	7.4	1.2	6.17
Lumber and wood products	5.0	1.2	4.17
Furniture and fixtures	3.5	0.7	5.00
Paper and allied products	8.4	1.9	4.42
Printing and publishing	5.3	1.1	4.82
Chemicals and allied products	13.3	4.7	2.83
Petroleum refining	20.9	5.2	4.02
Products of petroleum and coal	0.9	0.2	4.50
Rubber products	5.4	1.5	3.60
Leather and leather products	2.9	0.7	4.14
Stone, clay, and glass products	6.2	1.5	4.13
Primary nonferrous metals	7.3	1.7	4.29
Primary iron and steel	17.4	3.1	5.61
Fabricated metal products	13.9	3.1	4.48
Machinery	22.0	6.4	3.43
Electrical machinery	16.5	3.4	4.85
Transportation equipment	11.6	1.4	8.28
Motor vehicles and parts	25.6	3.4	7.53
Instruments	4.0	1.1	3.63
Miscellaneous manufactures	4.8	1.0	4.80

SOURCE: Federal Trade Commission and Securities and Exchange Commission.

[a] Annual sales divided by year-end working capital.

The ratio "sales per dollar of working capital" is used in comparative analysis. The financial position is more readily determined by the current ratio and quick ratio described in Chapter VII.

The working capital is also studied in relation to fixed assets and to capitalization, especially the funded debt and preferred stock. A good industrial bond or preferred stock is expected, in most cases, to be entirely covered in amount by the net current assets. The working capital available for each share of common stock is an interesting figure in common stock analysis. The growth or decline of the working capital position over a period of years is also worthy of the investor's attention.[1]

In the field of railroads and public utilities, the working capital item is not scrutinized so carefully as in the case of industrials. The nature of these service enterprises is such as to require relatively little investment in receivables or inventory (supplies). It has been customary to provide for expansion by means of new financing rather than out of surplus cash. A prosperous utility may at times permit its current liabilities to exceed its current assets, replenishing the working capital position a little later as part of its financing program.

The careful investor, however, will prefer utility and railroad companies that consistently show a comfortable working capital situation.

The working capital of a corporation is *increased* by (a) the amount of the net income, (b) the cash which flows from the annual provision for depreciation and depletion, and

---

[1] A severe test of a company's financial position is applied by using the current assets exclusive of inventory. These may be called the quick assets, and their amount, less current liabilities, would be known as the net quick assets. It is desirable to have an excess of quick assets over all current liabilities.

(c) by the funds raised through the sale of securities, and sometimes by the sale of noncurrent assets.

Working capital is *decreased* by the amount expended for new plant and equipment (or other noncurrent assets) and by dividends paid on preferred and common stocks.

United States Steel Corporation in its *Summary of Financial Operations* in 1953 gave the following detailed changes in working capital:

Working capital (December 31, 1952)	$326,555,376
Additions (during 1953)	
Net Income	222,087,840
Depreciation and Depletion	236,555,029
Proceeds of sale of plant	6,447,910
Proceeds of sale of bonds	4,984,195
Total additions	$470,074,974
Deductions (during 1953)	
Expenditures for plant and equipment	$342,432,637
Miscellaneous deductions	4,628,983
Dividends on preferred and common stock	103,548,945
Total deductions	$450,610,565
Increase during 1953	$ 19,464,409
Working capital (December 31, 1953)	$346,019,785

CHAPTER VIII

Current Ratio

ONE of the most frequently used figures in analyzing balance sheets is the ratio between current assets and current liabilities. This is usually called the current ratio, and is obtained by dividing the total current assets by the total current liabilities. For example, if the current assets are $500,000 and the current liabilities are $100,000, the current ratio is 5 to 1, or simply 5. When a company is in a sound position, the current assets well exceed the current liabilities, indicating that the company will have no difficulty in taking care of its current debts as they mature.

What constitutes a satisfactory current ratio varies to some extent with the line of business. In general, the more liquid the current assets, the less the margin needed above current liabilities. Railroads and public utilities have not generally been required to show a large current ratio, chiefly because they have small inventories and their receivables are promptly collectible. In industrial companies a current ratio of 2 to 1 has been considered a sort of standard minimum.

Many companies reduce their tax liabilities on the balance sheet by subtracting therefrom U.S. tax anticipation notes acquired for that purpose. Without this deduction, the current ratios would in many cases fall below 2 to 1. Where there are U.S. government securities on the asset side and accrued taxes on the liability side, the analyst would be justified in offsetting one against the other to arrive at an adjusted current ratio.

The current ratio should be generally analyzed further by separating out the inventory. It is customary to require that the cash items and the receivables together exceed all the current liabilities. This is the so-called "acid test." (There is a tendency now to apply the term "quick assets" to these current assets, exclusive of inventory). If the inventory is of a readily salable kind, and particularly if the nature of the

CURRENT AND QUICK RATIOS OF
UNITED STATES MANUFACTURING CORPORATIONS
December 31, 1953

	Current Ratio To 1	Quick Ratio To 1
All industries	2.3	1.27
Food	2.4	1.14
Tobacco manufacturers	3.7	1.75
Textile mill products	3.3	1.60
Apparel and finished textiles	2.3	1.22
Lumber and wood products	3.0	1.83
Furniture and fixtures	2.8	1.50
Paper and allied products	2.6	1.66
Printing and publishing	2.4	1.75
Chemicals and allied products	2.5	1.51
Petroleum refining	2.6	1.78
Products of petroleum and coal	3.0	2.00
Rubber products	3.1	1.71
Leather and leather products	3.3	1.66
Stone, clay, and glass products	2.5	1.40
Primary nonferrous metals	2.4	1.33
Primary iron and steel	2.0	1.16
Fabricated metal products	2.6	1.31
Machinery	2.6	1.29
Electrical machinery	1.9	1.02
Transportation equipment	1.5	0.37
Motor vehicles and parts	1.7	0.95
Instruments	2.2	0.81
Miscellaneous manufactures	2.3	0.89

SOURCE: Federal Trade Commission and Securities and Exchange Commission.

business makes it very large at one season and quite small at another, the failure of a company to meet this latter "quick asset test" may not be of great importance.

In every such case, however, the situation must be looked into with some care to make sure that the company is really in a comfortable current position.

The ratio of current assets excluding inventory to current liabilities may be called the "quick ratio." The appended table gives the current and the quick ratios at the end of 1953 for various industries.

CHAPTER IX

Cash

No USEFUL separation can be made between cash proper and the other "cash assets" or "cash equivalents," consisting of certificates of deposit, call loans, marketable securities, etc. For practical purposes the various kinds of cash assets may be considered interchangeable. In theory, a company should not keep any more cash assets on hand than are required for the transaction of its usual business plus a reasonable margin for emergency requirements. But many companies tend to hold more cash than the business seems to need. Much of this surplus cash is held in the form of marketable securities. The current return on these investments is usually small. They may yield substantial profits (or losses) due to market changes, but such operations are not properly part of the ordinary commercial or manufacturing business.

A shortage of cash is ordinarily taken care of by bank borrowings. In the usual case, therefore, a weak financial position is likely to be shown more through large bank loans than through insufficient cash on hand. During recessionary stages in the economy it is particularly important to watch the cash account from year to year. Companies frequently build up their cash account even during periods of operating losses by liquidating a large part of their other assets, especially inventories and receivables. Other concerns show a serious loss of cash or—what amounts to the same thing—a substantial increase in bank loans. In such periods the way in which the losses reflect themselves in the balance sheet may be more important than the losses themselves.

Where the cash holdings are exceptionally large in relation to the market price of the securities, this factor usually deserves favorable investment attention. In such a case the stock may be worth more than the earning record indicates, because a good part of the value is represented by cash holdings which contribute little to the income account. Eventually the stockholders are likely to get the benefit of these cash assets, either through their distribution or their more productive use in the business.

CHAPTER X

Receivables

THE relative amount of receivables varies widely with the type of industry and the trade practices in paying up accounts. Also, in certain lines of business, receivables are likely to vary with the conditions of bank credit; that is, when bank loans are hard to get the amount of receivables increases as the company extends more than the usual amount of credit to its customers.

As in the case of inventories, receivables should be studied in relation to the annual sales and in relation to changes shown over a period of years. Any sudden increase in receivables as a percentage of sales may indicate that an unduly liberal credit policy is being extended in an effort to sustain the volume.

The FTC-SEC 1953 report shows that 9,000 manufacturing companies used in their sample had receivables at year-end 1953 of $22.8 billion against annual sales of $265.9 billion. Receivables thus work out to 8.6% of sales, indicating that the accounts are being liquidated in about 30 days.

The accounts receivable require the most careful scrutiny in the case of companies selling goods on a long-term payment basis. This group includes department stores, credit chains, and mail-order houses. Farm implements, trucks, and office equipment are also sold on long-term credits. Much of this installment business is carried on through finance companies which advance funds against the notes or guarantee of the seller. In most cases the finance company exacts a repurchase agreement from the manufacturer. In these instances neither the receivable nor the debt appears directly on the balance sheet of the manufacturer, but is referred to in a footnote. In analyzing the balance sheet such discounted receivables should be given full consideration as the equivalent of both assets and liabilities.

CHAPTER XI

Inventories

INVENTORIES comprise goods held for sale or in process of manufacture, and materials and supplies used up in operating the business. For manufacturing companies the figure is generally broken down into categories of raw materials, work in process, and finished goods. It is ordinarily the largest of the current items and at year-end 1953 accounted for 46% of the current assets of U.S. manufacturing corporations.

The chief criterion of inventory soundness is the turnover, defined as the annual sales divided by the year end inventory.[1] The standards on this point vary widely for different industries. The range of variation among industries and a norm for individual lines is supplied in the accompanying table. The comparison of inventory turnover among companies within an industry will in many cases reveal an important competitive advantage which marks the leading companies in the group. But this fact in itself is not conclusive unless all the companies being compared are using the same basis for valuing their inventory.

The two important ways of calculating inventory values are known as "first-in, first-out" (FIFO) and "last-in, first-out" (LIFO). The difference between them turns on how the cost of the items on hand is calculated. This basic dif-

---

[1] The true turnover is found by dividing the inventory into the *cost of sales*, but it is customary to use the total sales instead of the cost of sales. This accepted turnover is thus always larger than the true figure.

INVENTORY TO TOTAL CURRENT ASSETS,
UNITED STATES MANUFACTURING CORPORATIONS

December 31, 1953

(*billions of dollars*)

	Current Assets	Inventory	%
All industries	$98.5	$44.9	46
Food	10.2	5.4	53
Tobacco manufacturers	2.6	2.2	85
Textile mill products	4.9	2.5	51
Apparel and finished textiles	2.1	1.0	48
Lumber and wood products	1.8	0.7	39
Furniture and fixtures	1.1	0.5	45
Paper and allied products	3.1	1.1	35
Printing and publishing	1.9	0.5	26
Chemicals and allied products	7.8	3.1	40
Petroleum refining	8.4	2.7	32
Products of petroleum and coal	0.3	0.1	33
Rubber products	2.2	1.0	45
Leather and leather products	1.0	0.5	50
Stone, clay, and glass products	2.5	0.9	36
Primary nonferrous metals	2.9	1.3	45
Primary iron and steel	6.2	2.6	42
Fabricated metal products	5.0	2.5	50
Machinery	10.5	5.2	50
Electrical machinery	7.0	3.3	47
Transportation equipment	4.4	2.3	52
Motor vehicles and parts	8.2	3.6	44
Instruments	2.0	0.9	45
Miscellaneous manufactures	1.8	0.9	50

SOURCE: Federal Trade Commission and Securities and Exchange Commission.

ference is generally illustrated by a company's coal pile. If the coal bought is piled on top and the coal used is taken from the bottom, we have a typical case of first-in, first-out. The old coal is used up first and the stock that remains would naturally be valued on the basis of the most recent purchases. But if we assume the coal used is taken off the top we would have the typical last-in, first-out situation. The coal on hand at the inventory date would represent some old or original purchase, and it could be valued at an unchanging price from year to year.

INVENTORY TURNOVER, UNITED STATES MANUFACTURING CORPORATIONS[a]

December 31, 1953

(*billions of dollars*)

	Net Sales	Inventory	Turnover Rate
All industries	$265.9	$44.9	5.9
Foods	42.6	5.4	7.9
Tobacco manufacturers	3.8	2.2	1.7
Textile mill products	13.0	2.5	5.2
Apparel and finished textiles	7.4	1.0	7.4
Lumber and wood products	5.0	0.7	7.2
Furniture and fixtures	3.5	0.5	7.0
Paper and allied products	8.4	1.1	7.6
Printing and publishing	5.3	0.5	10.6
Chemicals and allied products	13.3	3.1	4.3
Petroleum refining	20.9	2.7	7.7
Products of petroleum and coal	0.9	0.1	9.0
Rubber products	5.4	1.0	5.4
Leather and leather products	2.9	0.5	5.8
Stone, clay, and glass products	6.2	0.9	6.9
Primary nonferrous metals	7.3	1.3	5.6
Primary iron and steel	17.4	2.6	6.7
Fabricated metal products	13.9	2.5	5.6
Machinery	22.0	5.2	4.2
Electrical machinery	16.5	3.3	5.0
Transportation equipment	11.6	2.3	5.0
Motor vehicles and parts	25.6	3.6	7.1
Instruments	4.0	0.9	4.4
Miscellaneous manufactures	4.8	0.9	5.3

SOURCE: Federal Trade Commission and Securities and Exchange Commission.
[a] Annual sales divided by year-end inventory.

The LIFO method was introduced about 1941 in order to avoid marking up inventories to reflect the war-induced rise in the price level. It is widely felt that such gains in inventory values are illusory, and are likely to be followed by corresponding losses when the price pendulum swings downward. An additional object of importance is to avoid paying income tax on such questionable "profits."

However, the majority of companies have adhered to the older, and in some respects more natural, FIFO method. This has introduced a complication into statement analysis, particularly in the comparison of two companies using different bases of inventory valuation. As long as prices advance, the FIFO company will tend to show better earnings than the LIFO company, and its stated asset value will be correspondingly higher. These advantages are reversed when the price level turns downward, for then the FIFO company begins to show inventory losses which the other concern is spared.

The modest scope of this book prevents us from devoting adequate space to clarify so involved a subject. For a detailed discussion we can recommend *Survey of Accounting* by Leonard W. Ascher, published by Harper & Brothers, 1952.

CHAPTER XII

Current Liabilities (Notes Payable)

THE total amount of current liabilities is of interest only in relation to the current assets. You have already seen the importance of the current ratio (total current assets to total current liabilities), and the desirability of having the *quick* assets (exclusive of inventory) exceed the current liabilities.

The most important individual item among the current liabilities is that of notes payable. This generally represents bank loans, but it may also apply to certain trade accounts or borrowings from affiliated companies, or from individuals. The fact that a company has borrowed from the banks is not in itself a sign of weakness. Seasonal borrowings, which are entirely paid off after the close of the active sales period, are considered desirable from the viewpoints both of the company and the banks. But more or less permanent bank loans, even though they may be well covered by current assets, are likely to be an indication that the company is in need of long-term capital in the form of bonds or stock.

Where the balance sheet shows notes payable, the situation must always be studied with greater care than is otherwise called for. If the notes payable are substantially exceeded by the cash holdings, they can ordinarily be dismissed as relatively unimportant. But if the borrowings are larger than the cash and receivables combined, it is clear that the company is relying heavily on the banks. Unless the inventory is of unusually liquid character, such a situation may justify misgivings. In such a case the bank loans should be studied over a period of years to see whether they have been growing faster than sales and profits. If they have, it is a definite sign of weakness.

CHAPTER XIII

Property Account (Fixed Assets)

THE property account of a corporation includes land, buildings, equipment of all kinds, and office furnishings. These are often referred to as the "fixed assets," although many are quite movable, such as locomotives, floating equipment, small tools, etc. The proportion of the total assets taken up by the property account varies widely with different types of businesses. The property investment of a railroad is very large, while the property account of a finance company is likely to be an insignificant part of the total assets.

In nearly all companies the property account is carried at a conservative figure. The usual basis is actual cost less depreciation. Important amounts of new plant were written off in full by the accelerated amortization permitted under the tax laws during World War II, or are being similarly written down under present emergency legislation renewed in 1950. In many cases, also, plants were marked down in the depression of the 1930's to figures well below their cost.

Because of the frequent wide differences between book value and true value, stockholders should be supplied with more information regarding the present value of the property account than is contained in the ledger figures. We suggest that if the insured value of the plant and property were given as a footnote to the balance sheet, a much more informing picture of the plant account would be available to those who really own the assets.

Years ago it was not uncommon to find arbitrarily high values placed on the fixed assets—values which bore little relation to their actual cost or subsequent fair value. For example, the property account of the United States Steel Corporation was originally marked up or inflated by an amount in excess of $600,000,000. This gave the common stock a fictitious book value, and the epithet "watered stock" was commonly applied to inflated capitalization of this kind. (Subsequently the "water" was taken out of the property account of United States Steel by various kinds of special charges against earnings and surplus.) Present-day balance sheets are generally quite dependable as measures of the actual cash investment in property; differences, if any, lean toward the conservative side.

During the past forty years investors have come to pay less and less attention to the asset values shown by a company and to place increasing weight upon its earnings record and earnings prospects. This change in attitude was due in part to the frequent unreliability of the property-account figure, but it had separate justification in the fact that for the typical going business value does reside in earning power much more than in assets.

We think the pendulum has swung too far in the direction of ignoring balance sheet values. The property account should neither be accepted at face amount nor overlooked entirely. It deserves reasonable consideration in appraising the company's securities.

CHAPTER XIV

Depreciation and Depletion in the Balance Sheet

ALL fixed assets are subject to a gradual loss of value through age and use. The allowance made for this loss in value is known variously as depreciation, obsolescence, depletion, and amortization.

Depreciation applies to the ordinary wearing out of buildings and equipment. *Obsolescence* refers to an extra-rapid loss of value due to technological and similar changes. *Depletion* applies to the gradual removal of mineral and timber resources by turning them into products for sale. It is charged by mining enterprises, oil and gas companies, sulfur and lumber producers, and many others. *Amortization* is a general term applied to all deductions of the depreciation type, but it also connotes special kinds of charge-offs, e.g., "accelerated amortization" of defense facilities.

Allowances for depreciation, etc., appear both as a charge against earnings in the income account and as a deduction from the original value of the fixed assets in the balance sheet. In industrial companies the accumulated depreciation is subtracted directly from the fixed-asset account on the left side of the balance sheet. In utility and railroad accounting it often appears as an offsetting entry on the right or liability side.

The original cost of the property, without allowance for depreciation, is called the gross value. The figure after accrued depreciation, is called the net value. When property is retired or sold, its gross value is deducted from the property account and the depreciation accrued against it is taken out of the accumulated depreciation. This explains why the accumulated depreciation on the balance sheet may not increase in a given period by the full amount charged as amortization against earnings.

The more important aspects of the annual allowances for depreciation and depletion will be discussed in our section on the income account.

CHAPTER XV

Noncurrent Investments (Intermediate Assets)

MANY companies have important investments in other enterprises, in the form of securities or advances. Some of these investments are of the same sort as are made by the ordinary buyer of securities, namely, readily marketable bonds and stocks which are held for income or market profit, and which may be sold at any time. Such investments are usually listed among the current assets, as "marketable securities."

Other investments, however, are made for purposes related to the company's business. They consist of stocks or bonds of affiliated or subsidiary companies, or loans or advances made to them. A consolidated balance sheet eliminates the securities held in *wholly owned* (and often in *majority owned*) subsidiary companies, including instead the actual assets and liabilities of the subsidiaries as if they were part of the parent company. But the interest in *partly owned* subsidiary and affiliated enterprises may appear even in consolidated balance sheets under the heading of "noncurrent investments and advances."

These items are usually shown on the balance sheet at cost, though they frequently are reduced by reserves set up against them, and in fewer cases are increased to allow for accumulated profits. It is difficult to estimate the true value of these investments. Where it appears from the balance sheet that these items are likely to be of importance, a special effort should be made to obtain additional information regarding them.

Some investments stand midway between ordinary market-able securities and the typical nonmarketable permanent commitment in a related company. This intermediate type is illustrated by du Pont's enormous holdings of General Motors, or the large investment of Union Pacific in the securities of various other railroads. Such holdings will appear among the miscellaneous assets rather than the current assets, since the companies regard them as permanent investments; but for some purposes (e.g., calculating the quick assets per share of stock) it is permissible to regard them as the equivalent of readily marketable securities.

CHAPTER XVI

Intangible Assets

INTANGIBLE assets, as the name implies, are those which cannot be touched or measured. The most common intangibles are good will, trade-marks, patents, and leaseholds. Somewhat distinct from the concept of good will proper is the concept of going-concern value, the special profit-making character that attaches to a well-established and successful business. Trade-marks and brands constitute a rather definite type of good will, and they are generally referred to as part of the good-will picture. An investor should recognize a very strong distinction between good will as it appears—or more generally, fails to appear—on the balance sheet, and good will as it is measured and reflected by the market price of the company's securities.

The treatment of good will on the balance sheet varies among different companies. The most usual practice nowadays is either not to mention this asset at all, or to carry it at the nominal figure of $1. In some cases good will has actually been acquired at a definite cost in the original purchase of the business from its former owners, and it is then feasible to show the good will at cost in the same manner as other assets.

When one company acquires another, the purchase price frequently exceeds the current value of the assets of the acquired company. This excess is generally classified as good will and set up in the balance sheet as an asset to be written off against income over a period of years.

The modern tendency is not to ascribe any value to good will on the balance sheet. Many companies which started with a substantial good-will item have written this down to $1 by making corresponding reductions in their surplus or even their capital accounts.

This writing down of good will does not mean that it is actually worth less than before, but only that the management has decided to be more conservative in its accounting policy. This point illustrates one of the many contradictions in corporate accounting. In most cases the writing off of good will takes place after the company's position has improved. But this means that the good will is, in fact, considerably more valuable than it was at the beginning.

Patents constitute a somewhat more definite form of asset than good will. But it is extremely difficult to decide what is the true or fair value of a patent at any given time, especially since we rarely know to what extent the company's earning power is dependent on any patent that it controls. The value at which the patents are carried on the balance sheet seldom offers any useful clue to their true worth.

The "leasehold" item is supposed to represent the cost or money value of long-term leases held at advantageous rentals, i.e., rentals at lower rates than similar space could be leased. But in a period of declining real estate values, long-term leaseholds are just as likely to prove to be liabilities as assets, and the investor should be chary of accepting any valuation ascribed to that item.

In general, it may be said that little if any weight should be given to the figures at which intangible assets appear on the balance sheet. Such intangibles may have a very large value indeed, but it is the income account and not the balance sheet that offers the clue to this value. In other words, it is the earning power of these intangibles, rather than their balance-sheet valuations, that really counts.

CHAPTER XVII

Prepaid Expense and Deferred Charges

IN MOST balance sheets these two items appear together at the bottom of the list of assets. Because the amount of money they involve is small they are frequently excluded in computing asset values, such as the book value of stock or the tangible-asset protection for bonds.

Prepaid expense items differ somewhat from deferred charges in that the former are tangible assets and they may even properly be considered current assets. They represent amounts paid to others for services to be rendered in the future, and if these services are terminated in advance of completion, the items would have some residual or surrender value to the corporation.

Fire insurance premiums, for example, are frequently paid in advance for periods of five years. During the first year, one-fifth of the expense is charged to operations, with the remaining four-fifths listed in the balance sheet as prepaid expense. In each succeeding year, the asset is then reduced by one-fifth the original amount until the entire item is written off against operations. Prepaid rentals on property are handled in the same way. The American Institute of Accountants has suggested that prepaid-expense items (chargeable to earnings within a year) be included in the current assets—as the equivalent of accounts receivable—and they are now beginning to be treated in this fashion.

Deferred charges, in contrast to prepaid expense, represent

amounts paid for which no specific service will be received in the future but which are none the less considered properly chargeable to future operations. The expense of moving a plant might logically be amortized over a period of five years. Bond discount is usually written off over the life of the bond issue. Whatever the item may be, each year's expense is charged with a proportionate share and the balance is carried in the balance sheet as a deferred charge.

An item of increasing importance among deferred charges is the amount paid out as "past-service cost of pensions." This is the starting-up cost of a pension fund and in some cases is substantial. The U.S. Treasury Department has ruled that under tax regulations such amounts may be written off against future income over a period of not less than ten years. Sound and informing financial statements should, in the first year of this pension expense, charge one-tenth (or less) off immediately and show nine-tenths (or more) of the past service cost as a deferred charge to be deducted from income in subsequent installments. This method maintains reported income in line with income tax provisions—an important check point for analysts.

CHAPTER XVIII

Reserves

It is useful to divide reserves into three classes:

1. Liability reserves, which represent a more or less definite obligation.

2. Valuation reserves, which are offsets against the stated value of some asset.

3. Surplus or "voluntary" reserves, which merely set aside part of the reinvested earnings.

Reserves of the first class are set up for taxes, for accident claims and other pending litigation, for refunds to customers and similar obligations, and for certain future operating charges, such as relining blast furnaces. These are for the most part semicurrent liabilities; but in many cases they are separated from the current liabilities in the balance sheet and appear in an intermediate position.

The most important *valuation reserves* are those for depreciation and depletion, which we have already discussed. Another offsetting reserve is that for losses on receivables, or "reserve for bad accounts." This is deducted directly from the accounts or notes receivable and frequently the amount taken off is not stated.

A third important offset reserve is that for decline in inventories. In dealing with such a reserve it is essential to know whether it reflects a decline that has already taken place or merely one that may be expected. If the former is true, the inventory must be considered as definitely reduced by the amount of the reserve. But if the reserve is set up to take care of a possible *future* decline in value it must be viewed rather as a reserve for contingencies, which is in reality part of the reinvested earnings.

The same point may be made with respect to reserves against marketable securities and other investments. Here, too, it is important to know if they reflect a past and actual, or merely a possible, decline in value.

Contingency reserves and other similar reserves tend to make corporate statements confusing, because they obscure the time and effect of various kinds of losses. If in one year a company sets up a reserve for future decline in inventory value, it seems proper to take this reserve out of surplus, rather than charge it to earnings, since the loss has not actually been realized. But if in the next year a decline in inventory takes place, it seems proper again to charge this loss against the reserve set up for that contingency. It follows that the loss, although actually incurred, is not charged against income in any year, and to that extent, the earnings for the period have been overstated.

To avoid being deceived by these devices the analyst must examine both the income statement and the reinvested earnings over several years and make due allowance for any amount charged to surplus (reinvested earnings) or reserves which really represent business losses during the period.

Now and then the balance sheet contains items such as "reserve for plant improvement," "reserve for working capital," "reserve for preferred stock retirement," etc. Reserves of this sort represent neither a debt nor a definite deduction from any asset. They are clearly part of the surplus account. The purpose in setting them up is usually to indicate that these funds are not available for distribution to the stockholders. If this is so, such reserves may be considered "appropriated surplus." Since 1948, there has been a perceptible trend toward simplifying and rationalizing financial statements. Among the steps taken is a strong drive in the direction of eliminating reserves of various kinds from the balance sheet. The thinking on the subject may be summarized as follows: (1) valuation reserves should be deducted directly—as "allowances"—from the affected asset; (2) reserves which represent real or probable liabilities should be classified as current liabilities or as reserves for specified contingencies; (3) those of an indefinite nature should be returned to earned surplus. The published balance sheets of Chrysler Corporation are models in this respect, since they do not show a single "reserve."

CHAPTER XIX

Book Value or Equity

THE book value (or "asset protection") of a security is in most cases a rather artificial value. It is assumed that if the company were to liquidate, it would receive in cash the value at which its various tangible assets are carried on the books. Then the amounts applicable to the various securities in their due order would be their book value, or in the case of bonds and preferred stocks, their "asset protection." (The word "equity" is frequently used instead of book value in this sense, but it is generally applied only to common stocks and to speculative senior securities.)

As a matter of fact, if the typical company were actually liquidated, the value of the assets would probably be less than their book value as shown on the balance sheet. An appreciable loss is likely to be realized on the sale of the inventory, and a substantial shrinkage is usually suffered in the value of the fixed assets. In most cases the adverse conditions which would lead to a decision to liquidate the business would also make it impossible to obtain anywhere near cost for the plant and machinery. In recent years there have been exceptions to this rule, because the higher price level has created so wide a margin between reproduction cost and book value that sometimes the total assets can be liquidated at an actual profit.

The book value really measures, therefore, not what the stockholders could get out of their business (its liquidating value), but rather what they have put into the business, including undistributed earnings. The book value is of some importance in analysis because there may be some relationship between the amount invested in a business and its future average earnings or its realizable value. It is true that in many individual cases we find companies with small asset values earning large profits, while others with large asset values earn little or nothing. Yet in these cases some attention must be given to the book-value situation. For there is always a possibility that large earnings on the invested capital may attract competition and thus prove temporary; also that large assets, not now earning profits, may later be made more productive, or they may be merged, sold as a whole, or liquidated piecemeal for well above the depressed market level of the stock.

CHAPTER XX

Calculating Book Value

THE book value per share of a common stock is found by adding up all the assets (excluding intangibles), subtracting all liabilities and stock issues ahead of the common, and then dividing by the number of shares. In most cases the book values may be computed readily from the conventional published balance sheet.

As an alternative, it is sufficient to add together the common stock at par or stated value, the various surplus items, and the voluntary reserves, and to subtract any arbitrary items for intangibles. This will give the total common-stock equity, which is then divided by the number of shares.

Adjustment may be made, if desirable, to correct the stated liability for preferred stock. The proper calculation of this liability often presents a problem. The simplest rule to follow is to value stocks with preference claims at the highest of their par value, call price, or market price. Where there are preferred dividend arrears, these should be deducted as well in arriving at the book value for common. In the case of a high-coupon noncallable preferred, a "synthetic par value," e.g., the equivalent of a 5% dividend rate, may be more appropriate than any other measure. As an illustration, consider U.S. Steel 7% noncallable preferred carried in the balance sheet of the company at $360,281,100, representing 3,602,811 shares of $100 par value. A more realistic appraisal would be $140 a share, arrived at by capitalizing the 7% dividend at a 5% yield. On this basis the liability becomes $504,393,540, an increase of $144,112,-440. The use of this method would reduce the 1953 book value per share of U.S. Steel common from $76.38 to $70.86 as shown below.

ADJUSTED BOOK VALUE OF U.S. STEEL COMMON
December 31, 1953

Common stock	$ 870,325,200
Earned surplus	1,024,050,240
Reserves	100,061,875
Total	1,994,437,315
Additional preferred stock liability	144,112,440
Adjusted book value of common	1,850,324,875
Shares of common	26,109,756
Book value per share	$ 70.86

CHAPTER XXI

Tangible Asset Protection for Bonds and Preferred Stocks

THE U.S. Steel balance sheet may be used also to illustrate asset value computations for senior securities.

UNITED STATES STEEL CORPORATION CONDENSED BALANCE SHEET

December 31, 1953

Net plant	$1,970,002,353	7% preferred stock[a]	$360,281,100
Other assets	80,722,689	Common stock[b]	870,325,200
Investments	22,449,287	Bonds	64,475,699
Current assets	1,174,326,637	Current liabilities	828,306,852
Total assets	$3,247,500,966	Earned surplus	1,124,112,115
			$3,247,500,966

[a] 3,602,811 shares of 7% cumulative preferred ($100 par value).
[b] 26,109,756 shares of common. Stated value $33⅓ per share.

To find the tangible asset protection for the bonds, add up the par value of the bonds, the par value of the preferred stock, and the stated value of the common stock and surplus. If there are intangibles on the asset side they should be deducted from the total. The balance is then divided by the number of bonds outstanding.

Bonds	$ 64,475,699
Preferred stock	360,281,100
Common stock	870,325,200
Earned surplus	1,124,112,115
Total	$2,419,194,114
Number of bonds	64,476
Tangible assets per $1,000 bond	$37,520

As it happens, the small amount of debt outstanding in a corporation as large as U.S. Steel has produced asset protection for the bond issue in an unusually high amount. In the more typical case the coverage would be lower. In Bethlehem Steel Corporation, the asset protection per $1000 bond outstanding at year end 1953 came to $7,700.

To find the tangible-asset protection (or "book value") for the preferred stock, the bonds are excluded and only the figures for the preferred, common stock, and surplus are added. (Good will and intangibles would be deducted as in the case of the bonds). This total for U.S. Steel comes to $2,354,718,415, applicable to 3,602,811 shares of preferred, or $653.57 a share.

CHAPTER XXII

Other Items in Computing Book Value

IN CALCULATING the book value of a security, the various forms of surplus are all treated simply as surplus. For example, a company might show capital surplus, appropriated surplus, premium on stock sold, and profit and loss or earned surplus. These would all be added together and regarded as surplus.

In the chapter on reserves, it was mentioned that certain kinds of reserves are really a part of the surplus. These in-include reserves for contingencies (unless they relate to a definite and reasonably probable payment or loss of value); general reserve, reserves for dividends, reserves for preferred stock retirement, reserves for improvements, reserves for working capital, etc. Reserves for insurance may also properly be considered in the same class, but reserves for pensions are usually a true liability and should not be included as part of the surplus.

These reserves equivalent to surplus (sometimes called "voluntary reserves") which are really part of the surplus, should be added in with the surplus in figuring the book value. In finding the net book value all the intangibles should be deducted. Such deferred charges as organization expense and unamortized bond discount, should also be excluded.

CHAPTER XXIII

Liquidating Value and Net Current Asset Value

LIQUIDATING value differs from book value in that it is supposed to make allowance for loss of value in liquidation. It is obviously impractical to talk of the liquidating value of a railroad or the ordinary public utility. On the other hand, the liquidating value of a bank, insurance company, or typical investment trust (or investment holding company) may be calculated with a fair to high degree of accuracy; and if the figure is well above the market price this fact may be of real importance.

In the case of industrial enterprises, the liquidating value may or may not be a useful concept, depending on the nature of the assets and the capitalization setup. It is particularly interesting when the current assets make up a relatively large part of the total assets, and the liabilities ahead of the common are relatively small. This is true because the current assets usually suffer a much smaller loss in liquidation than do the fixed assets. In some cases of liquidation it happens that the fixed assets realize only about enough to make up the shrinkage in the current assets.

Hence the "net current asset value" of an industrial security is likely to constitute a rough measure of its liquidating value. It is found by taking the net current assets (or "working capital") alone and deducting therefrom the full claims of all senior securities. When a stock is selling at much less than its net current asset value, this fact is always of interest, although it is by no means conclusive proof that the issue is undervalued.

CHAPTER XXIV

Earning Power

OUTSIDE of the field of banks, insurance companies, and, particularly, investment funds, it is only in the exceptional case that book value or liquidating value plays an important role in security analysis. In the great majority of instances the attractiveness or the success of an investment will be found to depend on the earning power behind it. The term "earning power" should be used to mean the earnings that may reasonably be expected over a period of time in the future. Since the future is largely unpredictable, we are usually compelled to take either the current or past earnings as a guide, and to use these figures as a base in making a reasonable estimate of future earnings.

If there have been reasonably normal business conditions for a period of years, the average of the earnings over the period may afford a better index of earning power than the current figure alone. This is particularly true if the purpose is to determine whether a bond or a preferred stock constitutes a safe investment.

In the next few chapters the elements of an earnings statement will be discussed.

CHAPTER XXV

A Typical Public Utility Income Account

THE following income account of a public utility may be regarded as representative:

THE CLEVELAND ELECTRIC ILLUMINATING COMPANY
RESULTS OF OPERATIONS

Year Ended December 31, 1953

Revenues	
Sales of electric service	$88,057,978
Sales of steam service	3,285,092
Interest, rents, and other	480,984
Total revenues	$91,824,054
Expenses	
Operation	40,221,817
Maintenance	5,809,905
Provision for depreciation of plant and equipment	8,830,503
Provision for current taxes:	
Federal income	12,215,088
Other	7,006,373
Provision for future federal income taxes	843,000
Total expenses	74,926,686
Gross income	16,897,368
Deductions	
Interest on first mortgage bonds	3,631,250
Other	38,873
	3,670,123
Less: Interest during construction charged to property and plant	1,538,084
Total deductions	2,132,039
Net income	$14,765,329

STATEMENT OF EARNED SURPLUS

Balance beginning of year 1953	$38,338,066
Additions	
Net income for year 1953	14,765,329
Other credits	252,000
	53,355,395
Deductions	
Dividends declared	
Preferred $4.50 series ($4.50 per share)	1,147,444
Common ($2.60 per share)	8,690,001
Other debits	132,342
	9,969,787
Balance end of year 1953	$43,385,608

Some explanation of various items in this income account may be found helpful.

The division of total operating revenue by source shows that sales of electricity provide the bulk of revenue. Elsewhere in the report the sales of electricity to customers are classified by groups. This breakdown for 1953 was as follows:

Classification	Revenue	% of total
Residential	$27.0 million	30.7
Commercial	12.3 million	14.0
Industrial	41.5 million	47.2
Other	7.2 million	8.1

The expense item, operation, includes cost of fuel, labor, and administrative costs. Maintenance and depreciation are discussed in a later chapter.

The provision for future federal income taxes is explained in a footnote to the financial statements, as follows:

During the year the Company amortized defense facilities for income tax purposes, while continuing to record only normal depreciation in the regular accounts. As a result, Federal income taxes for 1953 were reduced by $843,000. This amount has been set aside as Earnings Retained for Use in the Business, Restricted for Future Federal Income Taxes. It will be used to offset the increase in taxes which will be incurred after the 5-year amortization period, as a consequence of our having claimed accelerated amortization in place of normal depreciation for income tax purposes.

This statement means that the company charged to earnings more income tax than it will actually have to pay for 1953, but properly so, since the difference will be payable in later years.

In calculating the fixed-charge coverage test (explained in detail in a subsequent chapter), we recommend that the item interest charged during construction be added back to gross income and that this amount be divided by the full interest requirements on the bonds.

CHAPTER XXVI

A Typical Railroad Income Account

ALL railroad reports are rendered on a uniform basis in accordance with the rules of the Interstate Commerce Commission. These reports are too elaborate to be presented here in full detail. The following condensation will show the more important elements in the income account.

ILLINOIS CENTRAL RAILROAD COMPANY
INCOME ACCOUNT

Year ended December 31, 1953

Total operating revenue			$308,373,591
Maintenance of Way and Structure	$ 45,235,865		
Maintenance of Equipment	50,647,143		
Other Operating Expenses	125,131,292		221,014,300
Net Operating Revenue			87,359,291
Income Taxes	25,923,000		
Other Taxes	21,680,722		47,603,722
Railway Operating Income			39,755,569
Equipment Rents (Net)	Dr. 7,078,695		
Joint Facility Rents (Net)	Cr. 262,873	Dr.	6,815,822
Net railway operating income			32,939,747
Other income			2,247,731
Gross income			35,187,478
Miscellaneous deductions			186,562
Available for fixed charges			35,000,916
Interest on funded debt	8,418,806		
Other charges	213,029		8,631,835
Net income			26,369,081

EARNED SURPLUS

Balance December 31, 1952		207,182,702
Credits:		
Net income	$26,369,081	
Other credits	1,581,647	
Total	27,950,728	
Debits:		
Sinking fund	1,038,570	
Preferred dividends	1,118,718	
Common dividends	6,110,901	
Other debits	452,459	
Total	$ 8,720,648	
Balance December 31, 1953		$226,412,782

The titles used above are those officially prescribed by the I.C.C. rules. Some of the more important items are frequently referred to under more popular names. For example:

Official title	*Popular title*
Total operating revenue	Gross earnings or gross revenue
Railway operating income	Net after taxes
Net railway operating income	Net after rents
Net income	Balance for dividends

Joint facility rents represent amounts paid (dr.) or received (cr.) for the use of terminal facilities or trackage in common with some other carrier. Equipment rents refer to payments made and payments received to and from other railroads (and private owners) for the use of rolling stock —freight and passenger cars and locomotives. Fixed charges include not only interest on bonds but also rentals for lines leased and operated as part of the system.

CHAPTER XXVII

A Model Industrial Income Account

WESTINGHOUSE ELECTRIC CORPORATION

Year Ended December 31, 1953

Income	
Products and services sold	$1,582,047,141
From other sources	11,902,581
Total income	1,593,949,722
Costs applicable to income	
Wages and salaries	568,967,627
Employee insurance and pensions	29,056,228
Social security taxes	11,393,639
Federal income and excess profits taxes	74,283,000
Other taxes	11,562,108
Materials and services from others	782,595,110
Interest and fees on debentures	10,784,185
Depreciation and amortization	28,751,095
Current provision for product guarantees	2,233,805
Total costs	$1,519,626,797
Net income for the year	74,322,925
Dividends paid:	
On preferred stock	1,900,000
On common stock	31,738,373
Total dividends	$ 33,638,373
Income retained in the business	$ 40,684,552

The above items are clearly defined and require no comment. It should be observed, however, that most income accounts of industrial companies are not so informing as this one.

CHAPTER XXVIII

Calculating Earnings

IN STUDYING a bond issue, the most important figure is the number of times the total interest charges (and equivalent) are earned. Charges of the same nature as bond interest (such as "other interest," rentals, amortization of bond discount) should be included therewith, and the number of times these "fixed charges" are covered should be computed. (In dealing with the bonds of holding companies it is usually necessary to consider the subsidiaries' preferred dividends as fixed charges, for these may have to be paid before there is any income available for the parent company's bonds.)

The coverage of interest or fixed charges is calculated, of course, by dividing these charges into the earnings available for them. The method of calculating earnings coverage is complicated by the question whether earnings before or after taxes should be used. Under tax laws interest payments on debt are deducted before arriving at the amount of profits subject to income tax. Increases or decreases in the rate of federal taxation would not therefore influence the ability of the company to meet the fixed charges on its bonds. Hence, earnings available for interest charges should properly be shown before deducting income taxes, and the coverage should be calculated from that figure.

In many corporate reports to stockholders, including nearly all railroads and public utilities, it is customary to reverse this order and to show the amount of earnings available for interest charges after deduction of income taxes. But the income tax figure is either shown or easily determinable, and the proper adjustment can readily be made by adding back the tax figure before computing coverage.

In the case of a senior bond issue it may be useful, on occasion, to compute the interest coverage without counting the charges on junior bonds. This is a *supplementary* figure, however, and must always be studied in conjunction with the total interest on all the issues outstanding (the "over-all" coverage), for ordinarily no bond issue can be strong if the enterprise as a whole is weak. It is never correct to calculate the coverage on a junior issue alone, after deducting from income the requirements of the senior issue. This may give very misleading results, and in the case of a small junior issue may indicate that it is safer than the senior issues, which is manifestly absurd.

Where there is a preferred stock issue not preceded by bonds, the earnings available for it may be shown either as dollars earned per share, or the number of times the dividends were covered. (The latter method has more to recommend it.) To find the preferred dividend coverage, simply divide the net income available for dividends by the dollar amount of the preferred dividend requirements.

However, if there are bonds outstanding, the preferred dividend coverage should be calculated only in conjunction with the fixed charges. In other words, you must calculate how many times the total of fixed charges plus preferred dividends was earned. It is common practice in these cases to calculate the preferred dividends separately, but that method is incorrect in the case of issues bought for investment and may give rise to seriously misleading results.

Consideration should be given the fact that preferred dividends (in contrast to bond interest) are paid after taxes and that changes in the corporate income tax rate may affect the ability of some companies to pay dividends. Under the present tax structure (1954) corporations are required to earn more than $2 before taxes to meet each dollar of preferred dividend requirements.

In the interest of simplifying the coverage test for preferred stocks preceded by bonds, we recommend that the following formula be used.

1. To the fixed charges add an amount equal to twice the preferred dividend requirements. (The doubling of preferred dividend is an arithmetic offset to compensate for the tax disadvantage of preferred stocks. The addition of such a tax component gives the same basic coverage for a preferred stock as the coverage *before taxes* of a corresponding bond).

2. The total of fixed charges plus the preferred dividends doubled is then divided into the amount available for fixed charges.

Common stock earnings are always shown as so much a share. They are computed after deducting preferred dividends at the full annual rate to which the issue is entitled (including the participating feature, if any), whether paid or not. (Back dividends on a preferred stock are not deducted from current earnings in figuring the amount available for the common, but the existence of such accumulated dividends must, of course, be taken into account).

EARNINGS CALCULATION 1953

	Cleveland Elec. Illuminating Co.	Ill. Central Railroad Co.	Westinghouse Elec. Corp.
Earnings available for fixed charges (before income tax)	$29,112,456	$60,693,916	$159,390,110
Total fixed charges	3,670,123	8,631,835	10,784,185
Fixed charge coverage	7.9×	7.0×	14.8×
Fixed charges and twice preferred dividends	5,965,011	10,869,271	14,584,185
Preferred dividend coverage	4.9×	5.6×	10.8×
Balance for common stock	13,617,885	25,250,363	72,422,925
Common shares outstanding	3,342,308	1,357,978	15,985,262
Earnings per common share	$4.07	$18.59	$4.53

CHAPTER XXIX

The Safety of Fixed Charges and Preferred Dividends

IN ANALYZING an investment-grade bond, the coverage of the fixed charges (before income tax) is the main criterion. In the case of a high-grade preferred stock, the comparable test is the coverage of the sum of twice the preferred stock dividends and the fixed charges.

Minimum required coverages should be set high enough to provide reasonable assurance of safety and should reflect variations in the inherent stability of the several major types of enterprises—public utilities, railroads, and industrials.

The following tests are recommended for investment grade bonds:

1. Average earnings, before income taxes, for a period covering the most recent seven years should equal, at least, the following multiple of fixed charges.

Type of enterprise	7-year average
Public utility	4 times
Railroad	5 times
Industrial	7 times

2. Alternatively, the earnings before income taxes of the *poorest year,* in the seven-year period, should equal at least the following multiple of fixed charges.

Type of enterprise	Poorest year coverage
Public utility	3 times
Railroad	4 times
Industrial	5 times

For investment-grade preferred stocks the same minimum figures as above are required to be shown by the ratio of earnings before income taxes to the sum of the fixed charges plus twice preferred stock dividends.

(The coverage figures suggested in our table are more stringent than those generally accepted. We recommend them nevertheless because experience suggests that investors in fixed-rate securities have suffered losses in the past which can be traced to acceptance of inadequate earnings protection.)

In an investment study of the income account, attention is given the following additional factors among others: (1) the operating ratio, a figure obtained by dividing the operating expenses by the total revenue or sales. This is a measure of the operating efficiency of the company and also of its ability to absorb reductions in volume or in selling price; (2) the ratio of fixed charges (or fixed charges and preferred dividends) to gross revenues; (3) the maintenance and depreciation charges; (4) the nature and amount of charges to surplus not included in the income account.

In studying these figures, comparisons should be made between various companies in the same field and for the same company in successive years.

CHAPTER XXX

Maintenance, Depreciation, and Similar Factors in the Income Account

A THOROUGHGOING analysis of an income account would take into consideration a number of factors which we have not space to discuss. But the subject of maintenance and depreciation must be given a fair amount of attention even in an elementary text such as this. By making excessive or insufficient allowances for these items the net earnings may readily be understated or overstated. It is important to remember that depreciation charges differ from other operating expenses in that they are not actually laid out in cash, but are book entries deducted from the profits on one hand and from the property account on the other. The tax law permits several different basic methods of calculating amortization, and different percentage rates may be admissible within the same method. In addition, companies frequently take greater or less depreciation in their published reports than is used in their tax returns.

The maintenance ordinarily represents a direct cash outlay similar to any other expense. In the case of industrial companies it is taken for granted that current maintenance is kept up to date, and the figure is not separately examined. But in railroading, where maintenance outlays absorb about a third of operating revenues, there is room for considerable variance in policy between one road and another and from year to year in the same road. Thus the "maintenance ratio" receives considerable emphasis in railroad analysis. This figure includes depreciation. In the case of public utilities, the maintenance charge or ratio is usually studied in conjunction with the separately stated provision for depreciation. (A total of about 16% of total operating revenues for the two items is normal here, and a wide departure from this figure will require special inquiry and perhaps a corrective adjustment to arrive at the true earning power.)

Some Highlights on Depreciation Policy

The most common depreciation method is the "straight-line" basis, which writes off the cost of the property (less expected salvage) in equal amounts each year over the estimated life of the asset.

Example: If machinery is installed at a cost of $100,000, with an expected life of eight years and a probable final salvage value of $10,000, the annual depreciation charge on a straight-line basis would be ⅛ × $90,000 ($100,000 less $10,000.) This gives $11,250 as the annual depreciation charge. Typical straight-line depreciation rates for important kinds of property include: buildings 2 to 5%, machinery 7 to 20%, furniture and fixtures 10 to 15%, automobiles and trucks 20 to 25% etc.

More liberal depreciation charges in the early years are permitted by the "declining balance" method. The initial annual rate may be as high as 1½ times the "straight-line" rate when applied to property constructed prior to 1954, and twice the straight-line rate against property completed after 1953. Using our previous example and applying it to new machinery purchased after 1953, the law would now allow charging off 25% of the undepreciated balance in each year. This would give successive annual deductions of

$22,500, $16,875, $12,657, etc. (Somewhat similar results would be obtained by a third permissive method known as the "sum of the digits.")

Furthermore, many facilities installed in World War II and since Korea have received "certificates of necessity" under which a certain portion of their total cost may be amortized completely by sixty equal monthly charges, i.e., in five years. This is known as "accelerated amortization." Many of the railroads have made equipment purchases subject to certificates of necessity. However, by an inexcusable ruling of the Interstate Commerce Commission on this matter, the carriers are required to overstate their true earnings. They may deduct from income only their "normal" depreciation on their facilities, and at the same time they must include in profits the taxes saved by applying the higher, accelerated rates.

A few companies (e.g., Chrysler) have been regularly charging more for depreciation than was allowed for tax purposes, but this will probably cease now that the law has been liberalized. Years ago it was frequent practice to *understate* the required depreciation, especially through the use by public utilities of the so-called retirement reserve method, but this too has now become rare.

We should mention that many corporation executives insist that depreciation charges should be large enough to *replace* the property worn out, and thus reflect increases in the price level (inflation). However, both the accounting profession as a whole and the tax laws insist that depreciation allowances should return only the original dollar cost of each asset.

The relationship between gross value of the property account and annual depreciation in 1953 for various manufacturing industries is shown in the appended table. Note that in most categories the figures vary between 4 and 6%.

UNITED STATES MANUFACTURING CORPORATIONS

Industry	Gross value of property, plant and equipment	Annual provision for depreciation and depletion	%
	(millions of dollars)		
Food	$ 10,027	$ 530	5.3
Tobacco manufacturers	358	16	4.5
Textile mill products	5,481	245	4.5
Apparel and finished textiles	689	46	6.7
Lumber and wood products	2,148	129	6.0
Furniture and fixtures	712	40	5.6
Paper and allied products	5,349	220	4.1
Printing and publishing	1,489	81	5.4
Chemicals and allied products	10,288	521	5.1
Petroleum refining	25,342	1,303	5.1
Products of petroleum and coal	424	20	4.7
Rubber products	1,873	100	5.3
Leather and leather products	467	26	5.5
Stone, clay, and glass products	3,828	181	5.3
Primary nonferrous metals	5,343	156	2.9
Primary iron and steel	12,830	424	3.3
Fabricated metal products	4,050	204	5.0
Machinery	7,069	391	5.5
Electrical machinery	3,961	239	6.0
Transportation equipment	1,805	75	4.1
Motor vehicles and parts	6,626	356	5.3
Instruments	1,226	71	5.8
Miscellaneous manufactures	1,229	67	5.4
Total of all industries	$112,614	$5,480[a]	4.9%

[a] Figures are rounded.

DEPLETION

Depletion, like depreciation, is a rather complicated affair. The company may ordinarily choose the most liberal of three possible methods, as applied to each separate depletable property, as follows:

In ordinary *cost depletion,* the company deducts that percentage of the cost of the property which the minerals extracted bear to the total estimated content. In *percentage depletion,* the company may deduct either a specified percentage of the gross income from the property (e.g., 27½% for oil, 12% for metal mines), or 50% of the net income, whichever is lower. In *discovery depletion*, the original cost of the property is marked up to a higher value established by the discoveries of mineral content after the purchase was made, and such larger value is amortized in lieu of cost.

DEVELOPMENT EXPENSE

Many oil and mining companies reduce their income taxes sharply by taking advantage of the privilege of charging against profits all development costs incurred each year. Moreover, most of them do not make this charge-off in their published statements. As a consequence, the reported earnings of such companies are overstated, in the same way as those of railroads, because of the way they are required to account for accelerated amortization.

In a thorough analysis, these methods of accounting for various kinds of amortization and development expense must be carefully examined.

CHAPTER XXXI

The Trend of Earnings

A CONSISTENT change in some important factor in the income account over a period of time is known as a trend. The most important trends for our purpose are those of interest and preferred dividends coverage, and of earnings available for the common stock; but these trends result in turn from favorable or unfavorable trends in the gross business, operating ratio, and fixed charges.

Obviously it is desirable that a company show a favorable trend in gross and net earnings. Senior securities of a company revealing a definitely unfavorable trend should not be bought for ordinary investment, even though the coverage may still be large, unless you are convinced that the trend will correct itself shortly. On the other hand, there is danger of attaching undue importance to a favorable trend, for this too may prove deceptive. In the case of investment issues it is well to require in every case that the *average* earnings show a satisfactory coverage for interest and preferred dividends.

In selecting common stocks it is proper to assign more weight to the indicated trend than in the purchase of senior issues, for a common stock can advance substantially in price if the trend continues. However, before purchasing a common stock because of its favorable trend it is well to ask two questions: (1) How certain am I that this favorable trend will continue? (2) How large a price am I paying in advance for the expected continuance of the trend?

CHAPTER XXXII

Common Stock Prices and Values

BROADLY speaking, the price of common stocks is governed by the prospective earnings and dividends. In the typical case the earnings will determine the dividends. The prospective earnings are, of course, a matter of estimate or foresight; and the action of the stock market on this point is usually controlled by the indicated trend. The trend is gauged in turn from the past record and current data, although at times the expectation of some quite new development will play a determining part.

The price of common stocks will depend, therefore, not so much on past or current earnings in themselves as upon what the security-buying public thinks the future earnings will be. (There are also important influences of a general or technical nature affecting stock prices—such as credit, political, and psychological conditions—which may not be closely related to any estimate of future earnings; but such influences will either eventually reflect themselves in the earnings or else prove to be quite temporary.)

In the ordinary case the price of a common stock is the resultant of the many estimates of what the earnings are going to be in the next six months, in the next year, or farther in the future. Some of these estimates may be entirely incorrect and some may be exceedingly accurate; but the buying and selling by the many people who make these various estimates is what mainly determines the present price of a stock.

The accepted idea that a common stock should sell at a

certain ratio to its current earnings must be considered more the result of practical necessity than of logic. The market takes the trend or future prospects into account by varying this ratio for different types of companies. Common stocks of enterprises with only slight possibilities of increasing profits ordinarily sell at a rather low price-earnings ratio (less than 12 times their current earnings); and the common stocks of companies with good prospects of increasing the earnings usually sell at high price-earnings ratio (over 15 times the current earnings). Thus two common stocks may show the same current earnings per share, may be paying the same dividend rate, and be in equally good financial condition. Yet stock A may be selling at twice the price of stock B, simply because security buyers believe that stock A is going to earn a good deal more than B next year and the years after.

When neither boom nor deep depression is affecting the market, the judgment of the public on individual issues, as indicated by market prices, is usually fairly good. If the market price of some issue appears out of line with the facts and figures available, it will often be found later that the price is discounting future developments not then apparent on the surface. There is, however, a frequent tendency on the part of the stock market to exaggerate the significance of changes in earnings both in a favorable and unfavorable direction. This is manifest in the market as a whole in periods of both boom and depression, and it is also evidenced in the case of individual companies at other times.

At bottom the ability to buy securities—particularly common stocks—successfully is the ability to look ahead accurately. Looking backward, however carefully, will not suffice, and may do more harm than good. Common stock selection is a difficult art, naturally, since it offers large rewards for success. It requires a skillful mental balance between the facts of the past and the possibilities of the future.

CHAPTER XXXIII

Conclusion

IN THE preceding chapters you have seen the various factors to be considered in reading financial statements. By an examination of the statements it is possible to form an opinion as to the present position and potentialities of the company. The asset value, the earning power of the company, the financial position as compared with other companies in the same industry, the trend of earnings, and the ability of the management to meet constantly changing conditions—all these factors have an important bearing on the value of the company's securities.

However, there are other factors outside the control of the company that are perhaps equally important in their influence on the value of its securities. The outlook for the industry, general business and security market conditions, periods of inflation or depression, artificial market influences, the popular favor of the type of security—these factors cannot be measured in terms of exact ratios and margins of safety. They can be judged only by a general knowledge gained by constant contact with financial and business news.

Knowledge of securities is becoming more and more widespread among the general public. While this development gives an increasingly wide field for security salesmen and customers' men, it demands more and more accurate knowlege on their part.

The investor who buys securities only when the market

price looks cheap on the basis of the company's statements, and sells them when they look high on this same basis, probably will not make spectacular profits. But, on the other hand, he will probably avoid equally spectacular and more frequent losses. He should have a better than average chance of obtaining satisfactory results. And this is the chief objective of intelligent investing.

PART II

Debits and Credits

THE understanding of financial statements will be aided by a brief outline of the bookkeeping methods upon which they are based. Bookkeeping, accounting, and financial statements, all are based on the two concepts of debit and credit.

An entry which increases an asset account is called a debit, or a charge. Conversely, an entry which decreases a liability account is also called a debit, or a charge.

An entry which increases a liability account is called a credit. Conversely, an entry which decreases an asset account is called a credit.

Since capital and the various forms of surplus are liability accounts, entries increasing these accounts are called credits, and entries decreasing these accounts are called debits.

Business books are kept by what is called the "double-entry system," under which every debit entry is accompanied by a corresponding credit entry. Hence the books are always kept in balance, meaning that the total of asset accounts always equals the total of liability accounts.

The ordinary operations of a business involve various income and expense accounts such as sales, wages paid, etc., which do not appear in the balance sheet. These operating or intermediate accounts are transferred (or "closed out") at the end of the period into surplus or into profit & loss (which is the name given to the surplus account that reflects operating results, dividends, etc.). Since income entries are equivalent to additions to surplus, they appear as credit or liability accounts. Expense entries, which are equivalent to deductions from surplus, appear as debit or asset accounts.

A "trial balance" shows all the various accounts as they appear on the books before the intermediate or operating accounts are closed out into profit & loss. The total of all debit balances must be equal to the total of all credit balances.

The appended simplified case history may be found use-ful as indicating how the operations of a company are en-tered on the books, then reflect themselves in the trial balance, and finally are absorbed into the balance sheet. (It is not to be expected that corporate bookkeeping can be adequately treated within the confines of this presentation. Hence, the reader may wish to replace or supplement the following material by reference to some standard textbook on accounting.)

At the beginning of the period Company X showed the following balance sheet:

Cash	$3,000	Capital stock	$5,000
Inventory	4,000	P & L surplus	2,000
	$7,000		$7,000

The ledger (the book in which the accounts are kept), from which the above balance sheet was taken, would appear as follows:

Cash		Inventory		Capital stock		P & L surplus	
Dr.	Cr.	Dr.	Cr.	Dr.	Cr.	Dr.	Cr.
$3,000		$4,000			$5,000		$2,000

During the period it sells on credit for $3,000 goods which cost it $1,800, and incurs various expenses, paid in cash, totaling $500.

The original entries, which are made in the journal, are as follows:[1]

Dr. Accts. Rec.	$3,000	Cr. Inventory	$1,800
Dr. Cost of sales	1,800	Cr. Sales	3,000
Dr. Expense	500	Cr. Cash	500

At the end of the period the above entries are transferred to the ledger, which will appear as follows:

Cash		Inventory		Accts. rec.		Sales	
Dr.	Cr.	Dr.	Cr.	Dr.	Cr.	Dr.	Cr.
3,000	500	4,000	1,800	3,000			3,000
	2,500 (to		2,200 (to				
	balance)		balance)				
3,000	3,000	4,000	4,000				
2,500		2,500					

Cost of sales		Expenses	Capital stock	P & L surplus
1,800		500	5,000	2,000

From the above the following trial balance would be taken off:

Cash	2,500	Capital stock	5,000
Inventory	2,200	P & L surplus	2,000
Accts. rec.	3,000	Sales	3,000
Cost of sales	1,800		
Expenses	500		
	10,000		10,000

The operating accounts are then closed out into profit & loss by the following transfer entries:

Dr. Sales	3,000	Cr. Profit & loss	3,000
Dr. Profit & loss	1,800	Cr. Cost of sales	1,800
Dr. Profit & loss	500	Cr. Expenses	500

It will be noted that these result in a net increase of $700 in profit & loss surplus, representing the profit for the period.

[1] Cost of sales is actually calculated by deducting closing inventory from opening inventory plus purchases. We use the above entry for the sake of simplicity

These entries eliminate the operating accounts. The ledger would now appear as follows:

Cash			Inventory			Accts. Rec.
3,000	500		4,000	1,800		3,000
	2,500 (to balance)			2,200 *(to balance)*		
3,000	3,000		4,000	4,000		
2,500			2,200			

Sales			Cost of sales			Expenses	
to P & L	3,000	3,000	1,800	1,800 to P & L	500	500 to P & L
	3,000	3,000	1,800	1,800	500	500

Capital stock		P & L surplus		
5,000	(from cost of sales)	1,800	2,000	
	(from expenses)	500	3,000	(from sales)
	To balance	2,700		
		5,000	5,000	
			2,700	

From the above ledger we would then have the following balance sheet, representing the condition of the company at the close of the period under consideration:

Assets		Liabilities	
Cash	2,500		
Inventory	2,200	Capital stock	5,000
Accts. rec.	3,000	P & L surplus	2,700
	7,700		7,700

PART III

Analyzing a Balance Sheet and Income Account By the Ratio Method

A NUMBER of the ratios used in the analysis of an industrial company's income account and balance sheet are presented herewith by use of the financial statements of the Bethlehem Steel Corporation for the year 1953. Various items in the balance sheet and income account are numbered. This will facilitate the explanation of the method of computing ratios. For example, margin of profit, the first ratio computed in this study is operating income divided by net sales. Operating income is item No. 4, and net sales is item No. 1. The method of computing margin of profit is expressed as $(4) \div (1)$, or in actual amounts, $\$292,579,606 \div \$2,082,025,788 = 14.0\%$.

BETHLEHEM STEEL CORPORATION

Income Account

Year Ended December 31, 1953

(1) Net sales	$2,082,025,788
(2) Costs of sales	1,715,708,312
Gross operating income	366,317,476
(3) Depreciation, depletion, and amortization	73,737,870
(4) Operating income	292,579,606
Other income	12,926,367
(5) Total income	305,505,973
(6) Fixed charges	10,558,136
Pretax income	294,947,837
Income taxes	161,000,000

(7)	Net income	133,947,837
(8)	Preferred stock dividends	6,537,209
(9)	Balance for common stock	127,410,628
(10)	Common stock dividends	38,331,768
	Reinvested earnings	89,078,860

CONSOLIDATED BALANCE SHEET

BETHLEHEM STEEL CORPORATION

December 31, 1953

Assets

Current assets

(11)	Cash		130,778,128
(12)	U.S. government securities		380,632,905
(13)	Receivables		173,938,687
(14)	Inventories		293,637,218
(15)	Total current assets		978,971,938
	Investments		34,416,245
	Other securities and receivables		16,947,354
	Deposits with federal and state agencies		5,160,852
(16)	Property, plant, and equipment	1,580,040,024	
(17)	Less depreciation and amortization	833,692,403	
(18)	Property account (net)		746,347,621
	Deferred charges		1,111,764
	Total		1,782,955,774

Liabilities

Current liabilities

	Accounts payable	90,216,967
	Accrued taxes	196,522,736
	Other expenses accrued	64,003,678
	Incentive compensation fund	20,941,505
	Note payable	204,000,000
	Dividends on preferred stock payable	1,634,302
(19)	Total current liabilities	577,319,188
(20)	Long-term debt	154,914,000
(21)	Accident compensation payable	12,000,000
(22)	Insurance reserve	30,000,000
	Capital and surplus	
(23)	7% cumulative preferred stock	93,388,700
(24)	Common stock	303,459,830
(25)	Surplus	611,874,056
	Total	1,782,955,774

Margin of Profit

Operating income divided by net sales.

Formula: (4) ÷ (1)

In this case: $292,579,606 ÷ $2,082,025,788 = 14.0%

Used to determine the operating efficiency, this ratio means that
for every dollar of sales, the company had 14 cents left after
paying all costs of operations. From this amount (plus other
income) must be paid bond interest, income taxes, and preferred and common dividends.

Earnings on Invested Capital

Net income plus fixed charges divided by the sum of the bonds,
preferred stock, common stock, earned surplus, and surplus
reserves.

Formula: (7) plus (6) ÷ the sum of (20) through (25)

In this case: $144,535,973 ÷ $1,205,636,586 = 11.9%

The per cent earned on invested capital is the true test of the
profitability of a business since it reflects not only the efficiency
of the operation (margin of profit) but the way in which the
enterprise is capitalized, as well. The ratio for Bethlehem Steel
in 1953 was about in line with steel companies in general, but
steel companies did better in that year than the average of
manufacturing corporations as a whole. These earned 10.5% on
capital stock and surplus in 1953, versus 13.3% for Bethlehem.

Fixed Charge Coverage

Total income divided by fixed charges.

Formula: (5) ÷ (6)

In this case: $305,505,973 ÷ $10,558,136 = 28.9 times

The recommended standards require that fixed charges be covered
7 times for the most recent 7-year period or at least 5 times in
the poorest of those 7 years. Total income in the years 1947-
1953 averaged $221 million, and in the poorest year—1947—
it came to $97.4 million. In the main test the average coverage
was 21 times, and in the poorest year test it was 9 times.

Preferred Dividend Coverage

Total income divided by the sum of fixed charges and twice preferred dividends.

Formula: (5) ÷ (6) plus (2 × 8)

In this case: $305,505,973 ÷ $23,632,554 = 12.8 times

The standards here are the same as for the fixed charge coverage test. For the 7-year period the coverage was 9.3 times, and in the poorest year it was 4.1 times. Since the stock passes the *average* test, its failure by a small margin to pass the alternative "poorest year" test is not significant.

Earnings per Share of Common Stock

Balance for common stock divided by the number of shares of common stock outstanding.

Formula: (9) ÷ (24, expressed as shares)

In this case: $127,410,628 ÷ 9,582,942 = $13.30

Depreciation as a Percentage of Cost of Plant

Formula: (3) ÷ (16)

In this case: $73,737,870 ÷ $1,580,040,240 = 4.67%

This means that the average life of all the items in the property account is taken at just under 22 years. The ratio of 4.67% (which includes accelerated amortization) is somewhat below the corresponding ratio for the steel industry, which came to 5.4% in 1953.

Depreciation as a Percentage of Net Sales

This ratio is used, at times, in comparisons of companies.

Formula: (3) ÷ (1)

In this case: $73,737,870 ÷ $2,082,025,788 = 3.5%

The Bethlehem Steel figure of 3.5% compares with a 1953 industry average of approximately 4%. This test is sometimes called the "service" or "usage" test. Increased sales resulting from heavier use of the plant could justify increased depreciation even though there was no additional investment in the gross amount of the plant account.

Common Stock Dividends as a Percentage of Earnings (Pay-Out")

Dividends paid on common stock divided by the balance for common stock.

Formula: (10) ÷ (9)

In this case: $38,331,768 ÷ $127,410,628 = 30%

The pay-out of earnings during 1953 was low for Bethlehem Steel in relation to the steel industry, where the per cent paid was 42%, and extremely low in relation to the prewar standard pay-out for industrials of 65% or 70%. If future average earnings of Bethlehem Steel do not fall below the 1953 figure, the investor could expect an increased dividend.

Inventory Turnover

Net sales divided by inventory.

Formula: (1) ÷ (14)

In this case: $2,082,125,788 ÷ $293,622,218 = 7 times.[1]

Bethlehem Steel's inventory turnover was slightly better than the industry average of 6.7 times.

Number of Days Average Account Receivable is Outstanding

Accounts receivable divided by net daily sales.

Formula: $(13) \div \dfrac{(1)}{365}$

In this case: $\$173{,}938{,}637 \div \dfrac{\$2{,}082{,}025{,}788}{365} = 30 \text{ days}$

The ratio is used to determine the credit policy of the company. A 30-day liquidation of receivables is in line with the policy prevailing among manufacturing companies in 1953.

[1] The real or physical turnover is found by dividing inventory which is carried at cost, into "cost of sales." Formula: (2) ÷ (14). In this calculation the turnover is 5.8 times.

Capitalization Ratios
Bond Ratio

Amount of bonds outstanding divided by the sum of the bonds, preferred stock, common stock, and surplus.

Formula: (20) ÷ (20 through 25 inclusive)

In this case: $154,914,000 ÷ $1,205,636,556 = 13.0%

Preferred Stock Ratio

Preferred Stock divided by the sum of the bonds, preferred stock, common stock, and surplus.

Formula: (23) ÷ (20 through 25 inclusive)

In this case: $93,388,700 ÷ $1,205,636,556 = 7.7%

Common Stock Ratio

The Sum of Common Stock and Surplus Divided by the Sum of Bonds, Preferred Stock, Common Stock, and Surplus.

Formula: (21 plus 22 plus 24 plus 25) ÷ (20 through 25 inclusive)

In this case: $957,333,886 ÷ $1,205,636,556 = 79.3%

To summarize:

The company is capitalized as follows: 13.0% in bonds, 7.7% in preferred stock, and 79.3% in common stock and surplus. The average industrial company should not have more than one-third of its capitalization in bonds, and at least half the capitalization should be represented by common stock and surplus. A similar calculation is frequently used which takes the market value of the preferred and common stocks for a period of years. This calculation is known as the stock-value ratio. The formula for bonds is: average market value of preferred and common stocks divided by the par value of the bonds. The formula for preferred stock is: average market value of common stock divided by the sum of the par value of the bonds plus the current market value of the preferred stock. Preferred and common stocks are valued at both the average price of the 5 previous years and at the current price; and the tests applied by using both price levels.

Current Ratio

Current assets divided by current liabilities.

Formula: (15) ÷ (19)

In this case: $978,971,938 ÷ $577,319,188 = 1.6 to 1

However, it is proper to offset accrued taxes by U.S. government securities held. By so doing the current assets become $782 million against current liabilities of $381 million, giving a revised current ratio of 2.06 to 1. This will meet the standard minimum requirement.

Quick Assets Ratio

Current assets less inventory, divided by current liabilities.

Formula: (15 − 14) ÷ (19)

In this case: $685,349,720 ÷ 577,319,188 = 1.1 to 1

This ratio exceeds the minimum requirement of 1 to 1.

Book Value of Common Stock

The sum of common stock and surplus divided by the number of shares of common stock outstanding.

Formula: (21 plus 22 plus 24 plus 25) ÷ (24, expressed as shares)

In this case: $957,333,886 ÷ 9,582,942 = $99.89 per share

It is customary to exclude intangible assets (good will, patents, etc.) from book value, i.e., they would be deducted from the sum of common stock and surplus before dividing by the number of shares.

Price-Earnings Ratio

Market price of the stock divided by earnings per share.

Early in 1954, Bethlehem Steel sold at 50; a figure corresponding to 3.7 times the $13.30 of earnings reported in 1953. A more suitable figure for investment analysis is the ratio of price to average earnings for a 7- to 10-year period. At 50, Bethlehem Steel was selling at 5.1 times its average 1947-1953 earnings of $9.81. This is a key ratio in determining the attractiveness of a common stock.

PART IV

Definitions of Financial Terms and Phrases

Accelerated Amortization. Extra-rapid depreciation (usually in a 5-year period) allowed on facilities constructed for war or defense purposes.

Acceleration Clause. Provision in a bond indenture whereby the principal may be declared due in advance of maturity, because of default in payment of interest or some other "event of default."

Accruals. Expenses charged against current operations but not requiring cash payment therefor until some future date. Thus bond interest may be accrued on the corporation's books each month, although it usually is paid only at 6-month intervals. Accruals may also refer to credit items, such as interest accrued on securities held.

Accumulative (Dividends). Same as *Cumulative.*

Adjustment Bonds. See *Income Bonds.*

"After Acquired Property" Clause. A provision in a mortgage indenture which places property subsequently acquired by the issuing company under the lien of the mortgage.

Amortization. The process of gradually extinguishing a liability, deferred charge, or capital expenditure over a period of time. Thus: (a) a mortgage is amortized by periodically paying off part of the face amount; (b) bond discount is amortized by periodically charging the earnings of each year during which the bonds are outstanding with their proper share of the total discount; (c) fixed assets are amortized by charges for depreciation, depletion, and obsolescence.

Arbitrage. Simultaneous completion of purchase and sale of securities (or commodities) at a profit-yielding price spread, made possible by: (1) existence of trading in such security or commodity in more than one marketplace; or (2) by existence of two separate securities with established terms of exchange from one to the other. Example of (1): simultaneous sale in the London market and purchase in New York of United States Steel at a spread sufficient to provide expenses plus a profit. Example of (2): simultaneous sale in the same marketplace of a common stock and the purchase of a bond or preferred stock currently convertible at a definite ratio into such stock, or of "rights" entitling the owner upon payment of a fixed amount of cash to acquire such stock, the spread in prices being sufficient to provide expenses plus a profit.

Articles of Association. A document similar to a charter or certificate of incorporation setting forth the terms under which an enterprise is authorized by the state to do business.

Asset Value. The same as definition (b) of *Book Value.*

Assets. The valuable resources, or properties and property rights, owned by a corporation. See *Capital Assets, Current Assets, Deferred Assets, Intangible Assets,* and *Tangible Assets.*

Audit. An examination of the financial status and operations of an enterprise, based mostly on the books of account, and undertaken to secure information for, or to check the accuracy of, the enterprise's balance sheet, income statement, and/or surplus statement. See also *Certified Report.*

Balance Sheet. A report of the financial status of an enterprise on a specific date. It lists in one column all the assets owned and their values, and in another column the claims of creditors and the equity of the owners. The two columns are always equal in total amount.

Basis. In the case of bonds, either the yield to maturity at a given price, as shown by the bond tables, or the price corresponding to a given yield to maturity.

Bills Payable. Technically, unconditional orders in writing upon the enterprise by another enterprise or person for the payment of a sum of money. In practice they usually represent bank loans payable.

Blue Chip Issues. A colloquial term applied to stocks which are of accepted investment merit, but have an abnormally high ratio of price to current earnings and dividends, and are popular market leaders.

"Blue Sky" Flotations. Originally applied to promotions of companies whose securities have no value. So named, because the purchaser receives no more than "blue sky" for his money. State and federal laws to prevent such flotations are now in force. Registration of securities under such laws is now called "blue-skying."

Bond. A certificate of debt which: (a) represents a part of a loan to a business corporation or governmental unit, (b) bears interest, and (c) matures on a stated future date. Infrequently a bond issue may fail to possess one of these characteristics. Short-term bonds (generally running for 5 years or less from date of issuance) are often called notes.

Bond Discount. In financial statements, represents the excess of the face value of a bond issue over the net amount received therefor by the issuing corporation. This discount usually is amortized over the life of the bonds. In popular investment parlance, represents the excess of the face value of a bond over its current market price. A bond "selling at a discount" is one selling at a price less than 100, or par. Conversely, a bond "selling at a premium" is at a price above par.

Bonds, Straight. Bonds conforming to the standard pattern, i.e., (a) unqualified right to repayment of a fixed principal amount on a fixed date, (b) unqualified right to fixed interest payment on fixed dates, (c) no further interest in assets or profits, and no voice in the management.

Bonds, Underlying. Bonds which have precedence over some other bond or bonds. They usually hold a first mortgage on property of a corporation which is also pledged under a junior general mortgage.

Book Value. (a) Of an asset: the value at which it is carried on the company's books. (b) Of a stock or bond issue: the value of the assets available for that issue, as stated on the books, after deducting all prior liabilities. It is generally stated at so much per share or so much per $1,000 bond. The accepted practice excludes intangibles in computing book value, which is thus the same as "tangible asset value."

Break-Up Value. In the case of an investment fund or a holding company issue, the value of the assets available for the issue, taking all marketable securities at their market price.

Business Man's Investment. An investment in which a certain amount of risk is recognized but is thought to be offset either by the chance of increased principal value or by a high income return. (In our view, the second consideration is generally unsound.) This term is based on the thought that a business man is both financially able to assume some risk and capable of following his investments intelligently.

Callable Feature. A provision of a bond issue by which it may be retired in advance of maturity at the option of the company, not the holder. The feature may provide for various prices at various times. Also applies to preferred stock.

Capital (of a business). (a) In the narrower sense, the dollar value assigned in the balance sheet to the various stock issues. (b) In a broader sense the investment represented by the stock issues and the surplus. (c) In a still broader sense the same as the foregoing but adding thereto all long-term obligations. See *Capitalization.*

Capital Assets or Fixed Assets. Assets of a relatively permanent nature which are held for use or income rather than for sale or direct conversion into salable goods or cash. The chief capital assets are real estate, buildings, and equipment, often referred together as "plant account" or "property account." Intangible assets, such as good will, patents, etc., are also capital assets.

Capital Expenditures. Expenditures or outlays of cash or its equivalent which are undertaken to increase or improve capital assets. Cf. *Revenue Expenditures.*

Capital Gain. Under tax law, a gain realized on the sale of securities, fixed property, or similar assets. If the asset had been held more than six months it is long-term gain and the income tax thereon is not more than one-half that on ordinary income.

Capital Gain Dividend. A dividend paid by a regulated investment company out of its long-term capital gains. Such dividends are treated by the recipient, for federal tax, as the equivalent of long-term capital gains of their own.

Capitalization. The aggregate of the various securities issued by a corporation, including bonds, preferred stock, and common stock. (It is sometimes a question of judgment whether a short-term obligation should be considered part of the capitalization or a noncapital current liability. If it falls due within a year, it is usually considered to be a current liability.)

Capital Structure. The division of the capitalization as between bonds, preferred stock, and common stock. Where common stock represents all or nearly all the capitalization, the structure may be called "conservative"; where common stock represents a small percentage of the total, the structure is called "speculative."

Capitalizing Expenditures. Certain kinds of expenditures may at the option of the company be treated either as current expense or capital expense. In the latter case the expenditure appears on the balance sheet as an asset, which is generally written off gradually over a period of years. Examples of such expenditures: intangible drilling costs (of oil concerns); development expense (in mines, and by manufacturing companies); organization expense; expense of floating bond or stock issues; etc.

Capitalizing Fixed Charges. Computing the principal amount of a debt which would carry the fixed charges in question. Method: divide the fixed charges by the assumed interest rate. Example: fixed charges of $100,000, capitalized at 4%, yield a principal value of

$$\frac{\$100,000}{0.04} = \$2,500,000.$$

Capital Surplus. See *Surplus*.

Cash Asset Value. The value of the cash assets (cash and cash equivalents) alone applicable to a given security issue, after deducting all prior liabilities. Ordinarily stated at so much per share or per $1,000 bond. The cash asset value of a stock is sometimes stated without deducting liabilities from the cash assets. This should be termed the "gross cash asset value," and it is a useful calculation only when the other assets exceed all prior liabilities.

Cash Equivalents. Assets held in place of cash and convertible into cash within a short time. Examples: time deposits, U.S. government bonds, and other marketable securities.

Certificate of Deposit. (a) A receipt for a security deposited with a protective committee or for some purpose such as a reorganization plan. These certificates of deposit, known as c/d's, are generally transferable and are dealt in as securities. (b) The same as a time deposit.

Certificate of Necessity. A document issued by the government entitling a company to charge accelerated amortization against a specified percentage of the cost of a new facility related to war or defense.

Certified Report. A corporate report (balance sheet, income statement, and/or surplus statement), the correctness of which is attested to by a certified public accountant as the result of an independent audit. In a thorough study it is advisable to study carefully the accountant's certificate appended to the report, since audits vary widely as to their scope, and a given audit may be subject to important limitations and reservations.

Charter. The certificate of incorporation or franchise received from the state, legally authorizing the corporation to carry on business as set forth under the grant of powers in the charter.

Civil Loans. Loans contracted by a government agency—national, state, or municipal.

Class A Stock. A name given to a stock issue to distinguish it from some other stock issue of the same company, generally called Class B or merely common. The difference may lie in voting rights, dividend or asset preferences, or other special dividend provisions. If there is a preference, it is generally held by the Class A shares, but other advantages may go either to the Class A issue or to the other common stock issue.

Closed-End Investment Company. An investment fund which does not offer new shares continuously nor undertake to redeem shares on demand. Thus its capital remains relatively fixed, but its shares may sell in the open market at a varying percentage of the applicable net asset value.

Collateral Trust Bonds. Bonds secured by other securities (either stocks or bonds) deposited with a trustee. The real investment merit of these bonds depends upon either or both of (1) the financial responsibility of the company issuing them, and (2) the value of the deposited securities.

Consolidation. A combination of two or more companies into one, to form a new company. See *Merger.*

Consolidated Statement. A corporate report (balance sheet, income statement and/or surplus statement) that combines the separate statements of the corporation and its subsidiaries. Such consolidated reports eliminate all intercompany accounts, and show the entire group of companies as if it were a single enterprise.

Contingent Liabilities. Liabilities indefinite as to either their amount or their occurrence. Examples: amounts involved in law suits or tax claims; liabilities under a guarantee.

Contingency Reserves. Reserves set up out of earnings or surplus to indicate a possible future loss or claim against the corporation, the likelihood of which is open to considerable question (e.g., possible future decline in the market value of inventories or marketable securities owned). In most cases they may be regarded as part of the surplus, but occasionally indicate *probable* as well as merely possible losses or claims.

Controlled Company. A company whose policies are controlled by another through ownership of 51% or more of its voting stock.

Conversion Parity or Conversion Level. That price of the common stock which is equivalent to a given quotation for a convertible issue, or vice versa. For example, if a preferred stock is convertible into 3 shares of common stock and sells at 90, the conversion parity for the common would be 30. If the common is selling at 25, the conversion parity for the preferred would be 75. This may also be called the *conversion value* of the preferred stock.

Conversion Price. That price of the common stock equivalent to a price of 100 for a convertible bond or a convertible preferred stock of $100 par value. For example, if a $1,000 bond is convertible into 40 shares of common stock, the conversion price of the common is $25 a share.

Conversion Privilege. See *Convertible Issues.*

Convertible Bonds. Bonds which are convertible into other securities at a prescribed price or ratio *at the option of the holder.* Usually convertible into the common stock of the corporation, but sometimes convertible into preferred stock, or even into other bonds. The holder is in the position of a creditor of the corporation with the privilege of additional profits if the enterprise is successful.

Convertible Issues. Securities which may be exchanged for other securities in accordance with provisions of the indenture (bonds), or the charter or bylaws (stock).

Credit. See *Debit & Credit.*

Cumulative Deductions Method. A method of computing bond interest coverage which takes into account only the interest on bonds of prior or equal rank to the issue being considered. Interest on bonds of junior rank is ignored by this method. This method should be used, if at all, only as a secondary test, supplementing the over-all method. See *Over-All Method.*

Cumulative Preferred Stock. Preferred stock entitled to dividends at a fixed rate and entitled to receive all such dividends not paid in previous years before the common stock can receive any payment. Some issues are cumulative only to the extent that dividends have been earned but unpaid in any year. (Suggested title for these: earned-cumulative issues.)

Cumulative Voting. An arrangement whereby each share of stock may cast as many votes for one director as there are directors to be elected. Its effect is to permit a substantial minority to elect one or more directors. Mandatory in some states (e.g., Illinois, Michigan) and specified by the bylaws of some corporations in other states.

Current Assets. Assets which either are cash or can be readily turned into cash or will be converted into cash fairly rapidly in the normal course of business. Include cash, cash equivalents, receivables due within one year, and inventories. (Slow-moving inventory should properly be excluded from current assets, but it is not customary to do so.)

Current Asset Value. The value of the current assets alone applicable to a given security, after deducting all prior liabilities. Ordinarily stated as so much per share or so much per $1,000 bond.

Current Liabilities. Recognized claims against the enterprise which are considered to be payable within one year.

Debentures. Obligations of a corporation secured only by the general credit of the corporation. Have no direct lien on specific property of the corporation. (Sometimes applied, with no special meaning, to a preferred stock issue.)

Debit & Credit. Bookkeeping terms to describe types of accounts and entries to accounts. Entries to the left side of an account are called debits, and accounts which normally have left-side balances (asset accounts and expense accounts) are called debit accounts. One debits an account to record an increase in an asset, a decrease in a liability, or an expense. Entries to the right side of accounts are called credits, and accounts with right-side balances (liability accounts, owners' equities accounts, and revenue or profit accounts) are called credit accounts. One credits an account to record a decrease in an asset, an increase in a liability, or a revenue or profit.

Deed of Trust. See *Indenture.*

Deferred Assets, or Deferred Charges. Bookkeeping assets representing certain kinds of outlays which will eventually be treated as expenses. They are not immediately charged to any expense account because they are more properly chargeable against future years' operations. Include unamortized bond discount, organization expense, development expense, and prepaid advertising, insurance, and rent. These latter prepaid expenses are sometimes called prepaid assets.

Deferred Maintenance. The amount of repairs that should have been made to keep plant in good running condition, but that have been put off to some future time. This measure of equipment neglect usually does not appear in the corporate reports, although its existence frequently is suggested by maintenance expenditures drastically lower than those of earlier years. This is most readily noticeable in the income accounts of railroads.

Deficit. When appearing in the balance sheet, represents the amount by which assets fall short of equaling the sum of liabilities (creditors' claims) and capital stock. When appearing in the income statement, usually represents the amount by which revenues fell short of equaling expenses and charges. An "operating deficit" means a loss *before* deducting fixed charges. "Deficit after dividends" is self-explanatory.

Depletion. The reduction in the value of a wasting asset due to the removal of part of that asset, e.g., through mining ore reserves or cutting timber.

Depletion Reserve. The valuation reserve reflecting the total depletion to date of the assets to which it pertains (usually mineral or timber resources). Deduction of this reserve from the corresponding balance sheet asset indicates the corporation's valuation of what remains of the asset, i.e., its net value.

Depreciation. The loss in value of a capital asset, due to wear and tear that cannot be compensated for by ordinary repairs, or to allowance for the asset's becoming obsolete before it wears out. The purpose of the bookkeeping charge for depreciation is to write off the original cost of an asset by equitably distributed charges against operations over its entire useful life. (When in any year more is charged on the books for depreciation than is reinvested in plant, the excess may be called "unexpended depreciation.")

Depreciation Reserve. The valuation reserve reflecting the total book depreciation to date, and therefore indicating the expired portion of the useful life, of the assets to which it pertains. A depreciation reserve of $200,000 against a $1,000,000 asset indicates, not that the asset's present resale value is $800,000, but rather that about 20% of the asset's useful life is believed to have expired.

Development Expense. (a) The cost of developing manufacturing or other processes or products to make them commercially useable. New enterprises frequently treat such items as deferred assets; established and successful enterprises more frequently treat them as current expense. (b) The cost of opening up an oil or mining property—in most cases treated as a deferred asset.

Dilution. From the standpoint of a convertible issue, an increase in the number of common shares without a corresponding increase in the company's assets. Most convertible issues are protected against this contingency by an "antidilution clause," which reduces the conversion price in the event of dilution.

Diversification. Spreading the risk of investment by dividing the funds to be invested among a number of issues. An investment fund may diversify among different industries, or—less effectively—among different companies in the same industry; or geographically. Applies also to the kinds of business carried on.

Dividend Coverage. The number of times a dividend has been earned in a given period. Preferred dividend coverage should properly be stated only as the number of times the combined fixed charges and preferred dividends have been earned. Common dividend coverage is stated separately, but the figure must be viewed in the light of the senior obligations.

Dividend Yield. A percentage figure, found by dividing the dividend rate in dollars by the market price in dollars. Example: If a stock paying \$4 annually sells at \$80, the dividend yield is:

$$\frac{4}{80} = 5.00\%.$$

Dividend Scrip. (a) Certificates issued as a scrip dividend (see *Scrip Dividends*). (b) Fractional shares of stock, received as a stock dividend. These fractional shares usually are not entitled to dividends or voting power until combined into full shares.

Divisional Liens. A term usually applied to bonds secured by a mortgage on a section of minor length of a railroad system. If the mileage covered by the lien is a valuable part of the system, the specific security is good. If the mileage covered by the lien is of small value to the system the specific security is poor.

Earned Surplus. See *Surplus*.

Earning Power. Properly, a rate of earnings which is considered as "normal," or reasonably probable, for the company or particular security. It should be based both upon the past record, and upon a reasonable assurance that the future will not be vastly different from the past. Hence companies with highly variable records or especially uncertain futures may not logically be thought of as having a well-defined earning power. However, the term is often loosely used to refer to the average earnings over any given period, or even to the *current* earnings rate.

Earnings Yield. The ratio of the market price to the annual earnings. Example: a stock earning $6 annually and selling at 50, shows an earnings yield of 12%. See also *Price-Earnings Ratio.*

Earnings Rate. The annual earnings stated as so much per share, or (less frequently) as a percentage of the par value.

Earnings Ratio. See *Price-Earnings Ratio.* The relationship between the annual earnings and the market price, in which the price is expressed as a multiple of the earnings. In the example under "earnings yield," the price-earnings ratio would be stated as $8\frac{1}{3}$ to 1.

Effective Debt. The total debt of a company, including the principal value of annual lease or other payments which are equivalent to interest charges. (Such may not appear as part of the funded debt.) The effective debt may be calculated by capitalizing fixed charges (see definition) at an appropriate rate. Where long-term bond issues carry an abnormally high or an abnormally low coupon rate, the effective debt may be thought of as higher or lower than the face value.

Effective Par. In the case of preferred stocks, the par value which would ordinarily correspond to a given rate of dividend. Found by capitalizing the dividend in dollars at an appropriate rate, say 6%. Example: the effective par of a $2.40 preferred stock would be $\frac{2.40}{0.06} = 40$. Useful when dealing with no-par preferred issues or those having a par out of line with the dividend rate.

Equipment Obligations or Equipment Trust Certificates. Bonds, usually maturing serially, secured by a lien on the rolling stock of a railroad. There are two methods generally used to protect the creditor: (1) the Philadelphia Plan, now almost universal (title to equipment rests in hands of trustee until all certificates have been paid off, at which time title is transferred to the corporation); (2) the New York Plan (a conditional bill of sale is given to the corporation which issues the certificates; after the certificates have been paid off the corporation receives unqualified title).

Equipment Rentals. Sums paid by one railroad, generally to another railroad, for the use of rolling stock. These payments are on a per diem (per day) basis, in accordance with a standard schedule. The amounts paid or received appear in the railroad income statement immediately after the tax item.

Equipment Trust. An arrangement relating to the ownership or control of equipment (usually rolling stock of railroads) by a trustee, under which equipment trust certificates or bonds are issued. Often used to mean equipment trust certificates.

Equity. The interest of the stockholders in a company, as measured by the capital and surplus. Also the protection afforded a senior issue by reason of the existence of a junior investment.

Equity Securities. (a) Any stock issue, whether preferred or common. (b) More specifically, a common stock or any issue equivalent thereto through having a virtually unlimited interest in the assets and earnings of the company (after prior claims, if any).

Equity, Trading on the. When a business man borrows money for his business, to supplement his owned capital, he is said to be "trading on the equity." The underlying idea is that more profit can be made on the borrowed capital than the interest paid thereon. The phrase is sometimes used to mean specifically the extreme case where most of the capital is borrowed and only a small amount is owned.

Expenditures vs. Expenses. Expenditures are outlays of cash or the equivalent; frequently they involve no concurrent charge against operations or earnings (e.g., capital expenditures). Expenses are costs, i.e., charges against current operations or earnings; frequently they involve no concurrent cash expenditure (e.g., accruals, depreciation).

Factor of Safety. A method of stating fixed charge coverage, as the percentage of the balance after fixed charges to the fixed charges. Example: earnings available for interest, $175,000; interest charge, $100,000. Factor of safety equals

$$\frac{175,000 - 100,000}{100,000} = 75\%.$$

Factor of safety equals (interest coverage − 1) × 100%. (This term is becoming obsolete.)

FIFO . . . . First-In-First-Out. The usual way of determining cost of inventory on hand. Sales are deemed to be made against the earliest acquired items; hence inventory remaining represents those latest acquired.

Fiscal Year. The 12-month period selected by a corporation as the basis for computing and reporting profits. Usually coincides with the calendar year (i.e., ends December 31) but often differs from it. Many merchandising companies' fiscal years end January 31, to facilitate inventory taking after the close of the most active season; while some meat packers' fiscal year ends October 31, for the same reason.

Fixed Assets. See *Capital Assets*.

Fixed Charges. Interest charges and other deductions equivalent thereto. These include rentals, guaranteed dividends, subsidiary preferred dividends ranking ahead of parent company charges, and amortization of bond discount (the annual allowance to write off discount on bonds sold). Ordinarily building rents are not considered fixed charges, but are included in operating expenses.

Floating Assets. Same as current assets.

Flush Production. In the oil industry, the large production yielded by new oil wells during the first period of their life. This lasts a short time and is succeeded by a "settled production" at a much smaller rate. In analysis it is important not to consider the earnings from flush production as permanent.

Foreclosure. The legal process of enforcing payment of a debt secured by a mortgage, by taking the properties which it covers and selling them. This may be done when the principal or interest on the mortgage is not paid.

Funded Debt. Debt represented by securities, i.e., by formal written agreements evidencing the borrower's obligation to pay a specified amount at a specified time and place, with interest at a specified rate. Includes bonds, debentures, and notes, but does not include bank loans.

Going-Concern Value. The value of an enterprise considered as an operating business, and therefore based on its earning power and prospects rather than on liquidation of its assets.

Gold Clause. A clause in virtually all bonds issued for many years prior to 1933, under which payment was promised in gold dollars of the same weight and fineness as existed when the debt was contracted. No longer legal since 1933.

Good Will. Intangible asset purporting to reflect the capitalization of excess future profits expected to accrue as a result of some special intangible advantage held, such as brand names, reputation, strategic location, or special connections. In practice, the amount at which good will is carried on the balance sheet is rarely an accurate measure of its true value. Now usually carried at $1.

Gross Income. Sometimes used as the equivalent of gross sales. More often represents an intermediate figure between gross sales and net income.

Gross Revenues or Gross Sales. Total business done, without deduction of costs or expenses.

Guaranteed Issues. Bonds or stocks which are guaranteed as to principal, interest, dividends, sinking fund, etc., by a company other than the issuer. Guarantees usually come about through lease of the property of the issuing company to another company, or to facilitate the sale of securities by one company which is controlled by another. The value of the guarantee depends upon the credit standing and earnings of the guaranteeing company; but a guaranteed issue may stand on its own feet, even though the guarantee itself is questionable.

Hedge. Usually, to make a commitment in commodities for future delivery, in order to avoid risk of price change in such commodity entering into the cost of goods already contracted for manufacture and sale. In stock market operations, to purchase a senior convertible issue and sell short the amount of common stock obtainable if conversion privilege is exercised (or other operations similar thereto).

Holding Company. A corporation which owns all or a majority of the stock of subsidiaries. The distinction sometimes made between a *holding company* and a *parent company* is that the latter is an operating company which also owns or controls other operating companies, whereas the holding company merely holds or controls operating companies.

House of Issue. Investment banking company engaged in under·· writing and distribution of security issues.

Idle-Plant Expense. The cost of carrying (maintaining and allowing for depreciation on) nonoperating manufacturing properties.

Income Account. A report of operations over a specified period of time, summarizing the revenues or income and the expenses or costs attributed to that period, and indicating the net profit or loss for the period. Frequently called the *profit & loss statement.*

Income Bonds. Bonds whose interest payment is dependent on earnings. In some bonds part of the interest is on a fixed basis and the balance is on an income or contingent basis. Income bonds are sometimes called adjustment bonds.

Indenture. The legal document prepared in connection with a bond issue, setting forth the terms of the issue, its specific security, remedies in case of default, duties of the trustee, etc. Also called the "deed of trust."

Intangible Assets. Capital (fixed) assets which are neither physical nor financial in character. Include patents, trade-marks, copyrights, franchises, good will, leaseholds, and such deferred charges as unamortized bond discount. These assets should be shown on the balance sheet at cost, if at all, but frequently are assigned purely arbitrary values.

Intercorporate Debt. Debt of one corporation to another corporation controlling it, controlled by it, or controlled by the same interests that control the debtor.

Interest Coverage. The number of times that interest charges are earned, found by dividing the (total) fixed charges into the earnings available for such charges (either before or after deducting income taxes).

Intrinsic Value. The "real value" behind a security issue, as contrasted with its market price or book value. Generally a rather indefinite concept; but sometimes the balance sheet and earnings record supply dependable evidence that the intrinsic value is substantially higher or lower than the market price.

Inventories. Current assets representing the present stock of finished merchandise, goods in process of manufacture, raw materials used in manufacture, and sometimes miscellaneous supplies such as packing and shipping material. Usually stated at cost or market value, whichever is lower.

Investment Company. The official name given to an enterprise which invests its capital in a varied list of securities, intending to give its bond- and stockholders the benefit of expert financial management and diversification. Formerly (and still often) called an investment trust. A good unofficial term is "investment fund." See *Closed-End Investment Company, Open-End Investment Company,* and *Mutual Fund.*

Joint and Several Guarantee. A guarantee by more than one party under which each party is potentially liable for the full amount involved if his associates do not meet their share of the obligation.

Joint Facility Rents. In railroad income statements, represent rentals paid (dr.) or received (cr.) for terminal facilities or other similar properties used jointly by several railroads.

Junior Issue. An issue whose claim for interest or dividends, or for principal value, comes after some other issue, called a senior issue. Second mortgages are junior to first mortgages on the same property; common stock is junior to preferred stock, etc.

Leasehold. The right to occupy a property at a specified rental for a specified period of years. To obtain a long-term lease at a favorable rental a cash bonus may be paid by the lessee to the lessor (owner), if it is a new lease, or to the former lessee, if the lease is taken over. The balance-sheet item "leaseholds" should represent only this cash consideration, and should be amortized over the life of the lease.

Leasehold Improvements. The cost of improvements or betterments to property leased for a period of years. Such improvements ordinarily become the property of the lessor (owner) on expiration of the lease; consequently their cost must be amortized over the life of the lease.

Leasehold Obligations. The obligation or liability, inherent in a leasehold, to pay a specified rental for a specified period of years.

Legal Investments. Securities which conform with the regulations set up by legislative enactment governing the investments made by savings banks and trust funds in a given state. Usually, the banking department of the state publishes annually a list of securities (commonly referred to as "legals,") considered eligible for investment by savings banks and trust funds.

Leverage. The condition making for wide changes in per share earnings and market value, arising from the fact that a company's common stock has relatively heavy fixed costs or deductions (interest and/or preferred dividends) ahead of it. Small percentage changes in gross earnings or operating costs, or total asset values in the case of investment funds, will affect the earnings and market price of the common stock in much greater ratio. A leverage stock usually sells at a small aggregate figure in proportion to the total amount of senior securities.

Liabilities. Recognized claims against an enterprise. In its common and narrower sense includes only creditors' claims, i.e., excludes the claims of owners represented by the capital stock, surplus, and proprietorship reserve accounts. In its broader sense, includes all items on the right side of the balance sheet.

Liability Reserve. A reserve or claim against an enterprise representing a liability the existence of which is unquestioned but the exact amount of which cannot as yet be determined (e.g., loss reserves of an insurance company).

LIFO . . . . Last-In-First-Out. A method of valuing inventory on hand intended to minimize inventory profits and losses. Sales are deemed to be made against the most recently acquired items. Hence inventory remaining represents those earliest acquired.

Liquid Assets. Same as current assets; but sometimes applied to current assets excluding inventory (quick assets).

Liquidating Value. The amount which would be available for a security if the business were wound up and the assets turned into cash. Is usually less than book value, because allowance must be made for shrinkage in the value of the various kinds of assets if sold during a short period.

Loading Charge. The premium above net asset value, generally from 6 to 8%, charged by open-end investment funds on the sale of new shares, to cover selling costs.

Maintenance. Upkeep and repair costs required to maintain plant and equipment in efficient operating condition.

Margin of Profit. Operating income divided by sales. Depreciation is usually included in the operating expenses, while income taxes are usually excluded. Nonoperating income received and interest charges paid are not included in arriving at the operating income.

Margin of Safety. In general the same as interest coverage, which appears above. Formerly used in a special sense, to mean the ratio of the balance after interest to the earnings available for interest. Example: If interest is covered $1\frac{3}{4}$ times, the margin of safety (in this special sense) becomes $\frac{3}{4} \div 1\frac{3}{4} = 42\frac{6}{7}\%$.

Marketability. The facility with which a security may be bought and sold. Good marketability requires a continuous close relation between bid and offering prices sufficient to permit ready purchase or sale in fair volume.

Merger. A combination in which one company absorbs one or more other companies.

Minority Interest. In a consolidated income statement, represents the interest or equity of the minority stockholders of a subsidiary in the earnings of that subsidiary. In a consolidated balance sheet, represents the interest or equity of these minority stockholders in the net worth of the subsidiary.

Mortgage, "Blanket." Usually the same as general mortgage. May be applied more specifically to a mortgage issue covering a number of separate properties.

Mortgage, General. A lien on all the fixed property of a corporation at the time of issuance, usually junior to underlying mortgages.

Mortgage, Guaranteed. A mortgage on real estate on which payment of principal or interest (usually both) is guaranteed by a mortgage guarantee company or a surety company. Sometimes the whole mortgage is sold with the guarantee attached; frequently one or more mortgages are deposited with the trustee, and "guaranteed mortgage certificates" are issued with the mortgage(s) as security.

Mutual Fund. An open-end investment company.

Negotiable Instruments. Certain kinds of property, e.g., currency, checks, promissory notes, acceptances, coupon bonds, title to which passes on delivery and cannot be attacked when in the hands of a holder in due course and in good faith. Stocks are not negotiable instruments; hence stolen certificates may be recovered from an innocent holder.

Net Current Assets (Working Capital). Current assets less current liabilities.

Net Quick Assets. Either same as above, or (preferably) net current assets excluding inventory.

Net Plant. See *Property Account.*

Net Worth. The amount available for the stockholders as shown by the books. Is made up of capital, surplus, and such reserves as are equivalent to surplus. It is ordinarily used to include intangible assets as they appear on the books, and to that extent differs from the book value of the stock issues.

Noncumulative Preferred Stock. Preferred stock subject to the provision that if dividends are not declared in any period, the holder loses all rights to dividends for that period. Where the dividends are cumulative to the extent earned, the issue stands midway between a straight cumulative and a straight noncumulative preferred.

Nondetachable Warrants. See *Warrants.*

Nonrecurrent Items. Earnings or deductions from some special source not likely to appear in subsequent years. Such items should be separated from the regular earnings or deductions in analyzing a report. *Examples of nonrecurrent earnings*: profit on sales of capital assets; special dividends from subsidiaries; profit on bond retirement; amount received in settlement of litigation; etc. *Example of nonrecurrent deductions*: loss on sale of capital assets; inventory write-off; idle plant expense (in some cases); etc.

Obsolescence. The loss of value of a capital asset resulting from new manufacturing developments or inventions which render the asset commercially unusable. Also, the accounting charge (usually part of the depreciation charge) to adjust for the probable future loss in value resulting from these causes.

Open-End Investment Company. An investment fund which by charter provision agrees to redeem its shares at net asset value (or slightly less) on demand. Nearly all these funds sell additional shares continuously, in most cases at a premium ("loading charge") above the net asset value.

Operating Ratio. In the case of railroads, the ratio found by dividing total operating revenue (or gross revenue) into operating expenses excluding taxes. In the case of public utilities, it is generally defined as the ratio of operating expenses, including taxes and depreciation, to the total revenue. Similarly in the case of industrials, except that some authorities do not include depreciation and most do not include income taxes in operating expenses.

Option Warrants. See *Warrants*.

Organization Expense. Direct costs of forming a new corporate enterprise: mostly incorporation fees and taxes and legal fees. May appear on the balance sheet as a deferred asset; if so, is usually written off against the first few years' earnings.

Over-All Method. The proper method of calculating bond interest or preferred dividend coverage. In the case of bond interest it means finding the number of times that *total fixed charges* are covered. In the case of preferred dividends it means finding the number of times that the aggregate of all *fixed charges plus preferred dividends* is covered. (In dealing with a preferred issue senior to another preferred issue, the requirements of the junior issue may be omitted.)

Parent Company. See *Holding Company*.

Participating Issues. Bonds (very infrequently) or preferred stocks which are entitled to additional interest or dividends, above the regular rate, depending either on (a) the amount of earnings, or (b) the amount of dividends paid on the common stock.

Plant Account. See *Property Account.*

"Pre-emptive Right." The right of shareholders to purchase additional shares or other securities (generally securities convertible into common stock) before these are sold to other purchasers. Pre-emptive rights are generally accorded stockholders under state laws, but may be waived in the charter or bylaws.

Preferred Stock. Stock which has prior claim on dividends (and/or assets in the case of dissolution of the corporation) up to a certain definite amount before the common stock is entitled to anything. See *Cumulative Preferred Stock, Noncumulative Preferred Stock,* and *Participating Issues.*

Premium on Bonds. The excess of the market price of a bond, or the amount received by the issuer, over its face value.

Premium on Capital Stock. The excess of cash or equivalent received by the issuer over the par value of capital stock issued therefor.

Prepaid Assets. See *Deferred Assets.*

Price-Earnings Ratio. Market price divided by current annual earnings per share. Example: stock selling at 84 and earning $7 per share has a price-earnings ratio of 12 to 1 (or is said to be selling at 12 times earnings).

Prior Deductions Method. An entirely improper method of calculating bond interest or preferred dividend coverage. The requirements of senior obligations are first deducted from earnings and the balance is applied to the requirements of the junior issue. See *Over-All Method.*

Prior Lien. A lien or mortgage ranking ahead of some other lien. A prior lien need not itself be a first mortgage.

Privileged Issue. A bond or preferred stock which has a conversion or participating right, or has a stock purchase warrant attached to it.

Profit & Loss Statement. See *Income Account.*

Profit & Loss Surplus. See *Surplus.*

Property Account. The cost (or sometimes, the appraised value) of land, buildings, and equipment acquired to carry on business operations. *Net property account* represents cost or appraised value of these assets less accrued depreciation to date, i.e., property account less depreciation reserve. The terms *plant* and *net plant* frequently are used with the same respective meanings, but sometimes exclude land or nonstationary assets such as delivery equipment.

Proprietorship Reserves. Reserves set up as segregations of surplus, which serve merely to earmark part of the stockholders' equity as not subject to distribution in the form of cash dividends. Include most contingency reserves and also reserves for sinking funds and plant extensions. Represent not liabilities, but equities.

Prospectus. A document describing a new security issue; especially, the detailed description which must be supplied to intending purchasers under the Securities Act of 1933.

Protective Committee. A committee, generally organized at the initiative of substantial holders of a given security, to act for all the owners of that security in important matters in difficulty or dispute. Most protective committees arise in connection with a corporate trusteeship (receivership) and deal with the question of reorganization. Others may develop merely because of differences of opinion on some basic policy; e.g., between certain stockholders and the management.

Protective Covenants. Provisions in a bond indenture, or charter provisions affecting a preferred stock, (a) which bind the company not to do certain things considered injurious to the issue or, (b) which set forth remedies in the event of unfavorable developments. *Example of (a)*: agreement not to place a lien on the property ahead of the bond issue. *Example of (b)*: the passing of voting power to the preferred stock if dividends are not paid.

Proxy. An authorization given by a security holder to someone else to vote his holdings for directors, or on some question put to vote.

Purchase Money Mortgages. Mortgages issued in partial payment for real estate or other property and having a lien on the property purchased. They are often used to circumvent the "after acquired property clause" in bonds which a company has previously issued.

"Pure Interest." The theoretical interest rate on a riskless investment. Varies with general credit conditions. The actual interest rate on a given investment is presumed to be made up of the pure interest rate, plus a premium to measure the risk taken.

Pyramiding. In stock market operations, the practice of using unrealized paper profits in marginal trading to make additional purchases. In corporate finance, the practice of creating a speculative capital structure by a series of holding companies, whereby a relatively small amount of voting stock in the parent company controls a large corporate system.

Qualitative Factors (in analysis). Considerations which cannot be stated in figures, such as management, strategic position, labor conditions, prospects, etc.

Quantitative Factors (in analysis). Considerations which can be stated in figures, such as balance sheet position, earnings record, dividend rate, capitalization setup, production statistics, etc.

Quick Assets. Sometimes (a) used to mean current assets, but (b) preferably, current assets excluding inventory.

Receivership. Operation of a company by an agent of the court, under direction of the court, usually arising from inability to meet obligations as they mature. There are technical differences between (a) an equity receivership, (b) a bankruptcy receivership, and (c) a trusteeship under Section 77 and Chapter 10 of the Bankruptcy Act as amended.

Red-Herring Prospectus. A preliminary prospectus for information purposes, so-called because each page contains a large red legend warning that the document is not final or binding.

Registration Statement. The forms filed by a corporation (or foreign governmental body) with the Securities and Exchange Commission in connection with an offering of new securities or the listing (registration) of outstanding securities on a national securities exchange. The prospectus, supplied to intending purchasers of a new issue, contains most, but not all, of the information given in the registration statement.

Regulated Investment Company. Under the tax law (Internal

Revenue Code) an investment fund which can avoid income tax on its ordinary income and capital gains by distributing these profits as dividends and by meeting various other statutory requirements. See *Capital Gain Dividend.*

Reserves. Offsets against total or specific asset values, set up on the books (a) to reduce or revalue assets, (b) to indicate the existence of liabilities, generally of uncertain amount, or (c) to earmark part of surplus for some future use. See *Valuation Reserves, Liability Reserve,* and *Proprietorship Reserves.* Properly speaking, *reserves* represent, not assets, but claims against or deductions from assets. Assets set aside to take care of reserves should be called reserve *funds.*

Restricted Shares. Common stock issued under an unusual agreement whereby they do not rank for dividends until some event has happened—usually the reaching of a certain level of earnings.

Retirement Expense or Retirement Reserve. (a) In the income account: the accounting charge, formerly used by many public utility concerns in lieu of depreciation, for accruing loss due to ultimate retirement (scrapping) of operating equipment. May take into account all equipment owned, in which case it would approximate normal depreciation charges. More commonly, takes into account only equipment likely to be retired within the next few years, and hence is usually lower than normal depreciation charges. (b) In the balance sheet: retirement reserve is a valuation reserve representing accrued retirement expense to date. Similar to depreciation reserve, for which it is supposed to be a substitute, but frequently represents a smaller proportion of the value of the pertinent assets than would a properly built up depreciation reserve.

Revenue Expenditures. Expenditures or outlays of cash or its equivalent which are undertaken to maintain asset values (e.g., repairs, but not improvements) or to obtain current revenue (e.g., raw material purchase, factory labor payroll). *Cf. Capital Expenditures.*

Right. A privilege accorded to the holder of each unit of an existing security to purchase new securities. Generally rights must be exercised within a short time, and the new security is offered at a price under the existing market. See *Warrant*.

Royalty. A payment made (a) for the use of a patent, (b) to the owner of oil or gas lands by those extracting oil or gas therefrom, or (c) to the author of a book, play, etc.

Scrip Dividends. Dividends payable in notes or other written promises to pay the amount involved in cash at a later date. The date may be fixed, or contingent on certain happenings, or entirely discretionary with the directors.

Seasonal Variations or Fluctuations. Changes in operating results due to the time of the year. Allowance must be made for these in interpreting the results shown over part of the year.

Seasoned Issues. Securities of established large companies which have been favorably known to the investment public for a period of years covering good times and bad.

Secular Trend. A long-term movement, e.g., of prices, production, etc., in some definite direction. Opposed to seasonal fluctuations or variations.

Segregation. Separation from a holding or operating company of one or more of its subsidiaries or operating divisions, effected by distributing stock of the subsidiary to the shareholders of the parent company.

Senior Issue. See *Junior Issue.*

Serial Bonds. A bond issue providing that certain portions thereof mature on successive dates instead of all at once. Serial maturities are usually spaced one year apart.

Short Sale. Sale of a stock which is not owned. Delivery to purchaser is arranged by borrowing the stock from an owner who receives as security cash in amount equal and kept equal to the market price. Upon ultimate purchase of the stock by the shortseller, the certificate thereby received is turned over to the lender and cash posted with him returned.

Sinking Fund. An arrangement under which a portion of a bond or preferred stock issue is retired periodically in advance of its fixed maturity. The company may either purchase a stipulated quantity of the issue itself, or supply funds to a trustee or agent for that purpose. Retirement may be made by call at a fixed price, or by inviting tenders, or by purchase in the open market. The amount of the sinking fund may be fixed in dollars, or as a percentage of the issue, or based upon volume of production or earnings.

Sliding Scale Privilege. A conversion or stock purchase privilege in which the price changes (almost always unfavorably to the senior issue) either with the passage of time or upon exercise of the privilege by a given amount of the issue.

Speculation. Financial transactions involving acknowledged risk entered into with the purpose of profiting from anticipated future events.

Split-Up. Division of a corporation's share capital into a greater number of share units, usually (in the case of shares having a par value) by reduction in the par value represented by each share. Thus a split-up might consist of issuance, in exchange for each share of $100 par common stock outstanding, of four new $25 par common shares. Sometimes the reverse procedure is resorted to, i.e., the share capital is consolidated into a fewer number of shares by issuing only a fraction of a new share in exchange for each old share outstanding. For lack of a better title, this is frequently referred to as a *reverse split or split-down.*

Stock-Value Ratio. (a) In the case of a bond, the ratio of the total market value of the capital stock of a corporation to the par value of its funded debt. (b) In the case of a preferred stock, the ratio of the total market value of the common stock issues to the total par value of all the bonds plus the total market value of the preferred stock.

Stated Value (of capital stock). Value at which no-par capital stock is carried on the balance sheet. May be a purely arbitrary or nominal amount, or the issue price, or the book value of the stock. (In some states, par-value shares may be given a stated value less than their par.)

Stock Dividends. Dividends payable in the form of stock of the declaring company, but not necessarily of the same class as the shares receiving the stock dividend.

Stock Purchase Warrant. See *Warrants.*

Straight Investment. A bond or preferred stock, definitely limited in interest or dividend rate, purchased solely for its income return and without reference to possible increase in value.

Subsidiary. A company controlled by another company (called the parent company) through ownership of at least a majority of its voting stock.

Surplus. The excess of the total net worth or stockholders' equity over the total of par or stated value of the capital stock and the amount of proprietorship reserves. At least part of this excess usually results from earnings retained in the business; this part frequently is labeled *earned surplus* or *profit & loss surplus*, to indicate its source. That part of surplus arising from other sources (e.g., write-ups of fixed asset values, write-downs of the par or stated value of capital stock issues, or sale of stock at a premium) frequently is labeled *capital surplus.*

Surplus Statement. A financial report summarizing the changes in surplus during the fiscal year (or other period). Shows surplus at beginning of period, plus net income for the period, less dividends declared, plus or minus any extraordinary credits to or charges against surplus. Final item of report, consequently, is surplus at end of period. Report also called *statement of surplus* and *analysis of surplus.*

Switching. The process of selling a presently owned security and replacing it by another, to gain some expected advantage.

Tangible Assets. Assets either physical or financial in character, e.g., plant, inventory, cash receivables, investments. See *Intangible Assets.*

Tax-Free Covenant. An agreement by a corporation to pay interest without deduction of federal taxes that may be required to be withheld by law, usually up to a certain maximum percentage. Such covenants are found only in bonds issued prior to 1934, and the amount paid by the issuer on behalf of the bondholder is limited to 2%.

Time Deposit. Money on deposit with a bank withdrawable at the end of a (short) period instead of on demand, and generally drawing interest.

Treasury Stock. Lawfully issued stock that has been reacquired by the corporation through purchase or donation.

Trend. A persistent change (e.g., of earnings) in a certain direction over a given period. Caution must be used in projecting a past earnings trend into the future.

Trustee. (a) One to whom the title to property has been conveyed, for the benefit of another party. Thus the trustee for a mortgage bond issue holds the mortgage (i.e., has conveyed to it the mortgaged property) for the benefit, primarily, of the bondholders. The trustee in bankruptcy holds title to the bankrupt's property (with certain exceptions) for the benefit primarily of the bankrupt's creditors. (b) A trustee may also assume obligations not connected with the direct holding of property, e.g., a trustee under the indenture of an unsecured (debenture) bond, or a person exercising voting rights under a voting trust.

Trust Fund. Funds held by a trustee for the benefit of another. Terms set forth by the creator of the trust govern the type of property in which the trustee may invest, whether restricted to "legal investments" or left to the discretion of the trustee.

Unamortized Bond Discount. That part of the original bond discount which has not yet been amortized, or charged off against earnings.

Underlying Bonds. See *Bonds, Underlying.*

Unexpended Depreciation. See *Depreciation.*

Valuation Reserves. Reserves set up (a) to indicate a diminution in present value of the assets to which they pertain, or (b) to provide for a reasonably probable failure to realize full value. Example of (a): depreciation and depletion reserves; reserve to reduce securities owned to market value. Example of (b): reserve for bad accounts.

Voting Trust. An arrangement by which stockholders turn over their voting rights (generally for directors only) to a small group of individuals called voting trustees. The original stock certificates are registered in the name of the voting trustees and held in trust, the stockholders receiving instead other certificates called "voting trust certificates," (abbreviation v.t.c.). Voting trusts generally run for five years. They usually give the v.t.c. holders all the privileges of the deposited securities, except that of voting.

Warrants. (a) Stock purchase warrants or option warrants. A right to purchase shares of stock, generally running for a longer period of time than the ordinary subscription rights given shareholders. These warrants are often attached to other securities, but they may be issued separately or detached after issuance. Nondetachable warrants cannot be dealt in separately from the security with which they were issued, and can be exercised only upon presentation with the original security. Option warrants are often issued in reorganizations or granted to management as additional compensation and incentive. (b) A name given to certain kinds of municipal obligations.

Wasting Assets. Tangible fixed assets subject to depletion through gradual removal in the normal course of operations of the business (e.g., metal, oil, or sulfur deposits; timberlands).

Watered Stock. Stock with real net asset value considerably less than its par or stated value, because some of the asset value included in the company's balance sheet is either fictitious or highly questionable.

When Issued. A term applied to dealings in securities proposed to be issued under some reorganization, merger, or new capitalization scheme. The full descriptive phrase is "when, as, and if issued." If the plan is abandoned, or changed materially, the "when issued" trades are void.

Working Capital. The net current assets. Found by deducting current liabilities from the current assets.

Yield. The return on an investment, expressed as a percentage of cost. *Straight yield* or *current yield* is found by dividing the market price into the dividend rate in dollars (for stocks) or interest rate (for bonds). It ignores the factor of maturity or possible call at a price higher or lower than the market. *Amortized yield or yield to maturity* (of a bond) takes into account the eventual gain or loss of principal value to be realized through repayment at maturity. Where a bond is callable before maturity, the amortized yield might be lower if it is assumed that call takes place. The true amortized yield should be the lowest shown on any assumption as to call.